The National Museum of Modern Art
Paintings & Sculptures

Open daily from 12 a.m. to 10 p.m.
except Tuesday (Saturday and Sunday:
from 10 a.m. to 10 p.m.)
75191 Paris Cedex 04
Tel.: 42 77 12 33

MUSÉES ET MONUMENTS DE FRANCE

PUBLISHED WITH THE SUPPORT OF THE FONDATION PARIBAS
COLLECTION DIRECTED BY PIERRE LEMOINE

THE NATIONAL MUSEUM OF MODERN ART

PAINTINGS & SCULPTURES

JEAN-HUBERT MARTIN
Director of the National Museum of Modern Art

FABRICE HERGOTT
Curator

CO-EDITION
MUSÉES ET MONUMENTS DE FRANCE
CENTRE GEORGES POMPIDOU

The collection Musées et
Monuments de France has
been created on the initiative
of the Fondation Paribas

Introduction

The National Museum of Modern Art is Europe's premier museum of modern and contemporary art, and houses one of the major public collections in existence. Its unique location within the Centre Georges Pompidou has made possible the popularization both of its own prestigious collection and, beyond the confines of the Museum itself, of modern art as a whole. The Museum has contributed to the spread of knowledge about twentieth-century art and is undoubtedly one of the mainsprings of the current interest in modern and contemporary art.

Although it has existed under its current name only since 1945, the Museum's history goes back to the early nineteenth century. 1818 saw the creation of the Musée Royal du Luxembourg. The strict application of the regulations of the Institut des Beaux-Arts, under whose auspices this museum functioned, meant that only those artists who enjoyed State backing had their works displayed there. Courbet, the Impressionists, the innovative artists active at the beginning of the twentieth century would have to wait several decades before even being tolerated and cautiously incorporated into the collections. For more than a century authorities and curators were content simply to persist in their hostile and contemptuous attitude towards what was to become known as modern art. The museum was resited on a number of occasions and was subsequently split, in 1922, into two museums, one housing the French Schools, and one the Foreign Schools, the latter being located in the Jeu de Paume. During the same period museums were being set up abroad which applied a much more daring acquisitions policy as far as the art being created in Paris was concerned. The New York Museum of Modern Art was established in 1929; its Curator, Alfred Barr, pursued an extremely active, positive policy in regard to the great living exponents of modern art and to their predecessors.

Just prior to the Second World War, the collections were still very poor in avant-garde works. Modern art secured representation chiefly through donations, since the authorities controlled the budget and did not allow the curators to make the purchases they wished to make. The situation changed radically with the advent of the Front Populaire, when the new team at the Ministry of Education (there was as yet no Ministry of Culture) removed the Institut's exclusive power to decide the content of the national collections. After much debate, it was agreed, as part of the arrangements for the Universal Exhibition of 1937, to site the Museum of Modern Art in the Palais de Tokyo. Important commissions from Robert Delaunay, Dufy (*La Fée Electricité*), Picasso (*Guernica*), and Calder fostered acceptance of these new forms of art. 'The rift between talent and the State' was nearing its end. But reconciliation took place under the burden of budgetary constraints.

The Museum of Modern Art was founded immediately after the war, and inaugurated in 1947. It housed a mixture of documents, decorative works, and works of art, and organized numerous temporary exhibitions. Gradually the works of applied art were withdrawn from the exhibition rooms. The Museum conveyed a tame picture of twentieth-century art, stressing the conventional aspect of French art and rejecting Expressionism, Dada, and a good proportion of abstract art. The exhibition rooms soon became too small, and in 1954 a system of rotation was adopted for display. During this period major works entered the collection as a result of donations. Picasso, Miró, Léger, Chagall donated works which they themselves chose for the Museum. These exceptional donations were followed up with, and complemented by, a number of bequests and gifts from the artists' families. Works by Brancusi, Dufy, Braque, Rouault, Laurens, Pevsner, Pougny, González, Delaunay, Kupka, Calder, Dunoyer de Segonzac, and Gaudier-Brzeska were acquired in this way. (This procedure continues today and has resulted in recent years in the acquisition of works by Lipchitz, Kandinsky, Duchamp-Villon, Seuphor — in 1977 — and, recently, the DBC collection.) The paucity of funds available discouraged purchases; in addition, decisions on the spending of these funds were made by the Council at the Louvre, which rejected any proposed acquisitions it considered too daring — for example, Mondrian, Klee, Wols, and the Nouveaux Réalistes. The rare purchases that did take place occurred at long intervals and were systematically divided between the great artists — this was how Picabia's *Udnie* was acquired in 1949. It was only ten years later that a more purposeful approach to acquisitions was adopted, resulting in the entry into the collections of the first works by Dubuffet and Giacometti. This was the period of transformations prompted by a new generation keen to see the creation of a second site, complementary to the Museum, where research could be carried out into the latest developments in art. It was in this spirit that in 1964 plans for a museum of the twentieth century were drawn up. These plans were not implemented immediately, but they were partially realized when the museum was transferred to the Centre Pompidou.

At the end of the 1960s the new curators sought, in their acquisitions programme, to take a greater interest in foreign artists. The creation of the CNAC (Centre National d'Art Contemporain) in 1967 was a definitive sign that thinking was now geared towards contemporary art and its support. The CNAC was a research and information centre that organized exhibitions and purchased works from living artists; it was later to merge with the Museum. In 1971 President Pompidou relaunched the plan for a new national museum of modern art, earmarking the Beaubourg plateau as a site for this. Various additional schemes took shape: the CCI (Centre de Création Industrielle), set up by the Musée des Arts Décoratifs; a large-scale public library (BPI); and a research centre for contemporary music (IRCAM). The end result was a multidisciplinary project centred around a number of shared areas. Located as it was in the heart of Paris, and open to the general public, the site was a hive of activity.

The setting-up of the National Museum of Modern Art in the Centre Pompidou in 1977 meant that from 1975-76 the collection could begin to expand, thanks to new budgets administered independently of the Louvre. For the first time in its history, the Museum moved out of the supervisory ambit of the Direction des Musées and acquired the kind of independence that had previously been lacking in its development. Its installation in a building which, within the first few days, welcomed quotas of visitors exceeding all expectations and thus immediately acquired an international reputation, led the Museum into the most prestigious period of its long history. From this time on, the Museum acquired considerable standing and was rigorously structured into various services. The quality and number of its contemporary works places it amongst the leading international public collections of twentieth-century art. Since 1981 the funds made available for acquisitions have been trebled. However, increases in prices for works of art have hampered attempts to make good the relatively poor representation of German Expressionism, Italian Futurism, and Neo-Plasticism.

The collection is currently displayed in the form of a grand chronological tour occupying the whole of the Centre's fourth floor. In addition, a selection of the contemporary works occupies part of the third floor (also the location of the Museum's cinema, which regularly shows films by artists and about art). Most of the exhibition areas were reorganized in 1985. The original open, flexible arrangement, matching the spirit of the building, has given way to a more monumental architectural environment. The number of works in the collection is currently nearing 30,000, including 14,000 drawings housed in the Cabinet d'Art Graphique created in 1970 and located on the second floor. The collection expands by an average of 1,000 works each year, whilst the number of works that can be permanently displayed is 850. The collection also constitutes a fund of works that can be lent out for the various exhibitions organized by other institutions all over the world (over 1,000 works left the Museum for this purpose in 1988). It also makes possible long-term loans to provincial museums.

The Museum welcomes about 3,000 visitors each day, often rising to over 5,000 on public holidays. A system of regular rotation ensures as far as possible a broad view of the collection, the administration and documentation of which is overseen by a highly specialized information service (SAGA), soon to be complemented by a videodisc service. This more detailed form of documentation on the Museum's works draws on the general documentation service located in the administrative offices on the second floor. These house one of the major collections of books on modern art, as well as an extremely rich set of archives, open to students and researchers. In the Museum's galleries an educational service informs visiting groups about the collections and about modern art in general.

The Museum's other major activity is the organization and mounting of a large number of temporary exhibitions. The most important of these take place in the Grande Galerie on the fifth floor, the more contemporary ones in the Galerie Contemporaine on the first floor. Photographic exhibitions take place on the ground floor. A large body of well-informed and attentive staff is at hand to welcome the public to these various areas and to ensure supervision.

Despite its remarkable growth and its lengthy period of maturation, the National Museum of Modern Art is still a long way from achieving perfection in its mission — a mission that is constantly evolving. Its traditional function is to select works by great artists and to put together collections; but part of its task is also to rediscover the age to which a work belongs and, with the help of artists and collectors, to recreate as far as possible the periods of artistic history that have succeeded one another since the start of the century — both abroad and in France — and to make these known. Modern art and contemporary art are highly mobile subjects of study. Perspectives change, develop, and adapt, like a living organism. Modern art is opening up to industry and to the art of non-Western societies, who are about to assume a permanent place in the global community and are changing our conception of the world.

JEAN-HUBERT MARTIN
Director of the National Museum of Modern Art

Fauvism

At the opening of the Salon d'Automne in 1905, the term 'Fauves' (wild beasts) was used pejoratively to describe a group of artists whose paintings caused a furore on account of their unusually intense colours. Painted for the most part during the summer of that same year, the pictures were in complete contrast to the prevailing artistic taste, which was a compromise between a style of art abounding in conventional proprieties flattering to the ruling bourgeoisie, and the use of a soft open-air light — the only feature of Impressionism to be tolerated. During the first few years of the century, the predominant technique amongst the small number of artists who followed the innovative trends set by Manet, Monet, and Pissaro, was that of Divisionism (or Pointillism) — the system of painting whose principles had been established by Seurat. The technique is based on the logical distribution of a limited number of colours, applied in small dots. In Seurat's case the use of optical mixtures had produced incomparable results, but it had the disadvantage of leaving very little scope for initiative by the artist, hamstrung as he was by the necessity of laboriously reconstituting his visual impressions. This led a number of artists united in their non-regimented use of colour — following the example of Gauguin and Van Gogh — to break through to a freer expression of their feelings.

At the infamous exhibition it was Matisse who was regarded as the ringleader. One of his paintings — *Woman with Hat* — unleashed derisive uproar amongst the public, who thought the bright colours used for the face an insult to the model, if not a grotesque error. Derain painted *The Suburb of Collioure* whilst staying there in the company of Matisse. In this canvas he managed by painting on a ground of intense grey to reproduce the luminosity of this little Mediterranean port. The picture recalls the skyless spatial organization and humour of the Japanese prints that were so admired at that time. Vlaminck, an exuberant character very close to Derain during this period, managed in his *Red Trees* to marry the rhythmical ranks of three-trunks along the slanting roadside in the foreground to a finely balanced distribution of high-toned complementary colours, thus creating a unified whole. Dufy, with his *Posters at Trouville*, adopts a different approach: the vivid colours are confined to the poster-clad hoarding on the road leading out of the town. The subject is a new one and is indicative of the impact that the great zones of colour created by street posters were to have on artists of the time. The urban landscape is gradually replacing nature. Grey streams of clouds and strollers flow past above and below the gleaming posters.

The discovery of the Fauves at the 1905 exhibition — which quickly became known as 'la cage aux fauves' (the wild beasts' cage) — was a revelation to Georges Braque. However, he himself was careful to marry the new movement's luminous vigour to the kind of technical rigour practised by Cézanne. He was to say of *Little Bay, La Ciotat* that it was 'a Fauve canvas that doesn't roar'. Its luminous intensity derives from the way the brushstrokes are arranged on the canvas, allowing the dazzling ground to shine through at numerous points. Earth is almost indistinguishable from sky, and the few topographical features depicted form an

MAURICE DE VLAMINCK
Paris, 1876 -
Rueil-la-Gadelière, 1958
The Red Trees, 1906
Oil on canvas
65 x 81
Purchased by
the Musées Nationaux, 1947
AM 2673 P.

7

RAOUL DUFY
Le Havre, 1877 - Forcalquier, 1955
Posters at Trouville, 1906
Oil on canvas
65 x 81
Purchased by the Musées Nationaux, 1956
AM 3417 P.

ANDRÉ DERAIN
Chatou, 1880 - Garches, 1954
The Suburb of Collioure, 1905
Oil on canvas
59.5 x 73.2
Purchased by the Musées Nationaux, 1966
AM 4367 P.

evanescent framework. Matisse's *Algerian Woman* is a late Fauve work. In comparison with the drawing, the colour is almost classical. The line of the face echoes that of the arms and endows the picture with a measure of volume which the colours alone are incapable of conveying. The pale, relaxed hands echo the brightness of the face, framed by a mass of dark hair. This painting appears to have been executed after Matisse's trip to Germany in the winter of 1908/9. It may be that it was influenced by German Expressionism, as a result of this first encounter between these two close, parallel artistic movements.

As in the case of 'Fauvism', the term 'Expressionism' was initially also a pejorative one. It was in Dresden, also during 1905, that the association called *Die Brücke* (The Bridge) was founded by a group of students from the School of Fine Arts. Their aim was to promote a kind of art that would provide a forum for an harmonious meeting of minds and a harmonious encounter between art and life. They revived the woodcut, which during the German Renaissance had been a popular means of disseminating works of art. Although their political concerns were close to those of the Fauves — bordering on anarchism — the Expressionists differed in their artistic approach in that they did not subsequently abandon pure colour. Cubism influenced them only in its initial stages, and the main element of it which they retained was its sculptural aspect, since they too were interested in primitive art. Ludwig Kirchner's *The Toilet — Woman at the Mirror* does not display the violent contrasts of colour typical of pre-war Expressionism. The distortions affect not so much the young woman's body as the objects that surround her. As she knots up — or combs out — her hair, she seems to be gathering together thoughts, which are then retransmitted to us by 'delayed action' via the mirror. This quasi-fantastical atmosphere is even denser in Nolde's *Still-life with Dancing Women*. A tiny cow in terracotta nibbles conscientiously at a bunch of tulips, whilst on a little picture hanging in a red interior half-naked women come bursting out as if on to a night-club stage, in a scene far removed from the usual serenity of still-lifes.

Fauvism and Expressionism were not confined to France and Germany. Artistic circles all over Europe seemed to be awaiting the first opportunity to jettison academic conceptions of art. These two movements reflected a feeling that was being manifested in much of Europe. In Russia, Chagall, Larionov, Goncharova, and Malevich were taking their inspiration from popular art, employing distortion, and painting in pure colours. Kandinsky and Kupka, having realized that colour alone is sufficient to structure space, paved the way for abstract art, without realizing how close they were to each other in their investigations. Mondrian followed up his landscapes in Fauve colours — where the Dutch horizon meets the vertical line of a cloud or steeple — with his own interpretations of Cubism, subsequently moving on to his 'grid' paintings. By taking liberties with its subject, Fauvism prepared the ground for Cubism and abstract art.

GEORGES BRAQUE
Argenteuil, 1882 - Paris, 1963
Little Bay, La Ciotat, 1907
Oil on canvas
36 x 48
Donated by Mme Georges Braque, 1963
AM 4298 P.

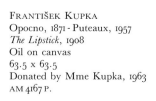

FRANTIŠEK KUPKA
Opocno, 1871 - Puteaux, 1957
The Lipstick, 1908
Oil on canvas
63.5 x 63.5
Donated by Mme Kupka, 1963
AM 4167 P.

MICHEL LARIONOV
Tiraspol (USSR), 1881 -
Fontenay-aux-Roses, 1964
The Blue Pig, 1907
Oil on canvas
65 x 75
Purchased by CNAC GP, 1976
AM 1976-16.

EMIL NOLDE
Nolde, 1867 - Seebüll, 1956
Still-life with Dancing Women, 1914
Oil on canvas
73 x 89
Purchased by the Musées Nationaux, 1963
AM 4228 P.

◁
ERNST LUDWIG KIRCHNER
Aschaffenburg (West-Germany), 1880
- Frauenkirch (Switzerland), 1938
The Toilet—Woman at the Mirror, 1912
Oil on canvas
100.5 x 75.5
Purchased by CNAC GP, 1979
AM 1980-54.

Matisse

It was at the age of 35, after some vacillation, that Henri Matisse found his artistic bearings. Colour, employed to its fullest extent, gave him the quality of expression that he was seeking. Under the influence of Cézanne, he adopted a rigorous approach to construction. Although he never abandoned figurative representation, it was construction, by means of which he linked drawing and colour-balance, which was the prime concern in his paintings: 'A colour does not', he said, 'attain its full expression until it is organized in such a way that the work creates its impression before the onlooker has had a chance to identify the subject'.

Interior, Bowl with Goldfish is a work whose subject nowadays seems so banal that the sophisticated nature of its composition is not immediately apparent. The sharp perspective is counterbalanced by the blue tone that bathes and softens the whole picture. The lines converge on the sunlit bank of a turquoise River Seine flowing beneath a pure summer sky. But it is the goldfish bowl that holds the observer's attention: two fish swim about in it as if suspended in the centre of the room. The light is intensely bright, casting shadows, but in the foreground it falls as if filtered through calm, opalescent water. The deliberately evoked sense of *bonheur de vivre* is a constant of all Matisse's works after 1905. He saw it as the crucial path to the onlooker's heart. In subtly balancing light and dark tones, he manages to create a sensation of colour that is the invisible yet tangible product of that contrast, like a sound articulated in the shape of the note. *French Window at Collioure* represents a purified stage in Matisse's investigations, whilst *Violinist at the Window*, opening out from its subject like the funnel of a megaphone, illustrates Matisse's development towards the representation of the physical presence of the human figure.

Decorative Figure on Ornamental Ground marks a crucial stage in Matisse's evolution. Decorative elements are incorporated into the painting and linked to the human figure in a technique that he would continue to use throughout his life. A naked model in hieratic pose sits on an oriental carpet in front of a wall papered in a rich floral motif. The dividing-line between the floor and the background of the painting is unclear, blurred by the various elements set around the young woman as if on a single continuous carpet on which she might be lying. The woman seems no more solid that these objects. A mixture of two and three dimensions is used, without its being possible to pin-point these precisely in the painting. The mirror, however, reflecting only a halo of blue light, maintains an evocative sensation of depth.

In contrast, the blue background in *The Dream* highlights the pink figure. The closed curl of the arm forms a protective ring around the cyclical movement of sleep. The face breaks through the ring like the sun emerging from its nocturnal journey, and the undulation of the fingers conveys a sense of fluidity. A work such as this cannot be viewed as a piece of symbolism: it is the result of observations made possible only through close proximity to the subject. Matisse sought to convey as accurate an impression as possible of his model. He

HENRI MATISSE
Le Cateau, 1869 - Nice, 1954
French Window at Collioure, 1914
Oil on canvas
116.5 x 89
Dation in payment for succession duties, 1983
AM 1983-508.

said his aim was to rediscover the individual rhythm of each figure and thus capture the likeness. There is a film showing the fourteen successive states of *The Rumanian Blouse*: begun as a 'realistic' representation, the painting ripens naturally, like a fruit, until it attains its full, symmetrical roundness, set against its background of scarlet.

The works done by Matisse during the last years of his life are made up of shapes cut out with scissors from sheets of gouached paper, which he then pinned on to the picture. He thus drew *in* the colour itself, uniting in a single gesture painting and colour. His gouached *découpages* were fixed in place when their final positions and shapes had been determined. Matisse's illness made it difficult for him to paint in any other way. *The Sad King* is one of his least decorative gouaches. Two musicians accompany a dancing woman. The enigmatic title would lead one to assume that the king is the central figure. Like King Lear, he has, so it would seem, abandoned his throne and retired from the world in contemplation and melancholy. The king is supposed to be the artist, and the dancer his model — an extremely important figure for Matisse. It may be that the king does not actually appear in the scene but is observing it.

HENRI MATISSE
Le Cateau, 1869 - Nice, 1954
The Dream, 1935
Oil on canvas
81 x 65
Purchased by CNAC GP, 1979
AM 1979-106.

13

HENRI MATISSE
Le Cateau, 1869 - Nice, 1954
The Rumanian Blouse, 1940
Oil on canvas
92 x 73
Donated by the artist to the State, 1953
AM 3245 P.

HENRI MATISSE
Le Cateau, 1869 - Nice, 1954
The Sad King, 1952
Cut-out gouache paper glued to canvas
292 x 386
Purchased by the State, 1954
AM 3279 P.

Bonnard

Because his precocious and innovative talent dates from the very start of his career, the earliest of Bonnard's works may be seen in the Musée d'Orsay, whilst the rest, which go well beyond the aims of Post-Impressionism, are displayed in the National Museum of Modern Art. In 1888 Bonnard belonged to the 'Nabis' group, which took a common interest in Gauguin's aesthetic tenets. These artists had come to realize that art is a creation of the spirit, for which nature merely serves as a pretext. Bonnard was given a nickname — 'Le Japonard' — because of his liking for the rather unbalanced

PIERRE BONNARD
Fontenay-aux-Roses, 1867 - Le Cannet, 1947
Studio with Mimosa, 1939-1946
Oil on canvas
127.5 x 127.5
Purchased by CNAC GP, 1978
AM 1978-732.

compositions that were a feature of Japanese prints — a liking that persists, even in his last works. He often juxtaposed different or successive views in the same picture. The landscapes and still-lifes painted in this way acquire added force from their habit of leaping out unexpectedly from the canvas, as if the artist had anticipated the movements of the eye in front of — one should properly say in — the real landscape or still-life. Bonnard even makes allowances for surprise effects and for the bedazzlement of the eye when it has not yet come to rest on the things it has just discovered. At the same time, his palette is rendered brighter and more intense by his special use of white. The result is an impression of lightness in which the objects do not arrest the observer's gaze but continually guide it away at a tangent — a tangent which, however, eventually leads the eye back to the centre, as if it were driven by a delighted and insatiable curiosity.

Studio with Mimosa, begun at Le Cannet in 1939, is one of the artist's last great compositions. It is a synthesis of all his research and, as is often the case with Bonnard, it represents a further step towards a vision free of all constraint. Under a spring sun the dazzling light from the mimosa blazes into the studio, the presence of which is alluded to by a single angle of wall in the foreground. The boundary between interior and exterior is scarcely perceptible and is rendered even more indistinct by the fine zig-zag lattice that spreads towards the back of the picture. Meanwhile, in the foreground, a blurred face moves across the canvas as in a snapshot.

PIERRE BONNARD
Fontenay-aux-Roses, 1867 - Le Cannet, 1947
Self-portrait in Bathroom Mirror, 1939-1945
Oil on canvas
73 × 51
Dation in payment for succession duties, 1984
AM 1984-698.

PIERRE BONNARD
Fontenay-aux-Roses, 1867 - Le Cannet, 1947
Flowering Almond Tree, 1946
Oil on canvas
55 × 37.5
Deposited by the Département des Peintures du Louvre, 1977
AM 1977 - DEP. 20.

Cubism

The use of colour, bearing no direct relation to the subject, gave the artist unprecedented freedom. However, the range of possible modes of expression remained restricted, and this meant that the task of conveying the sensation of reality was one that could only be accomplished with difficulty. Under the dual influence of primitive art and Cézanne, certain artists sought to achieve a more powerful representation of objects, without the forced use of local colour that had been employed by the Fauve painters. This marked the beginning of a veritable aesthetic revolution.

The instigators of this revolution were two young painters: Georges Braque, a native of Le Havre, and Pablo Picasso, a Spaniard who had settled in Paris. Both artists had seen items of African and Oceanic art in the studios of Matisse and Derain, and in the Musée du Trocadéro — objects which they were, perhaps, the only ones not to regard as 'cannibal fetishes'. In 1907 Picasso began work on a large-scale painting that was later to be given the coy title of *Les Demoiselles d'Avignon*. In fact the painting depicts a brothel-scene — which Picasso sets in the Carrer d'Avinyo in Barcelona — with a group of prostitutes welcoming their clients. To depict this highly emotionally charged subject, Picasso uses examples of stylization furnished by primitive art and presents the women from the point of view of the surprised, fascinated, and somewhat anxious men. As part of the peripheral work on this large-scale canvas — now in the Museum of Modern Art, New York — Picasso painted several small pictures, including a *Woman's Head*, thought to be one of the first studies for *Les Demoiselles d'Avignon*. The huge black almond-shaped eyes dividing the tapered head, the jutting nose set above the slender horizontal notch of a mouth — these are features of African statuary. Picasso transposes them from sculpture to painting without any loss of evocative power. The empty gaze emerging from a pallid but painted face is an image characteristic of the European *fin-de-siècle* still in search of its conclusion. There is a marriage of European and extra-European cultural references — the former give the face its structure, the latter are present in the stretching of the delicate skin over a powerful form dominated by pure lines. But the use of a style which Gauguin had been the first to incorporate into Western art does not of itself explain the birth of Cubism.

In 1908 Braque, fired by his admiration for Cézanne, went off to paint in the place where the 'Maître d'Aix' had created his landscapes. He returned from his trip with a series of paintings, including *The Viaduct at l'Estaque*. It was when he exhibited these the following autumn that there was talk of 'petits cubes' in relation to the stylized houses in the foreground; this led immediately to the coining of the word 'Cubism'. Following Cézanne's example, Braque applied colour right across the canvas. He spurned depth, with the result that his painting had the verticality of a wall. In the upper section the structure of the viaduct pulls the whole picture forward and throws up the buildings like stones in a torrent.

From this date onwards, Picasso and Braque

GEORGES BRAQUE
Argenteuil, 1882 - Paris, 1963
The Viaduct at L'Estaque, 1908
Oil on canvas
72.5 x 59
Dation in payment for succession duties, 1984
AM 1984-353.

between them established the essentials of Cubism. Braque was later to comment that they 'were like two mountain-climbers roped together'. By 1910 they were concentrating exclusively on light, because 'light and space impinge on each other'. Colour was spurned. In Picasso's *Guitarist* the facets are so dematerialized that they are scarcely identifiable. The artist scrambles them together and reconstitutes them to convey an accurate impression of his subject. The picture is therefore not an imitation of reality but a creation in its own right. Braque and Picasso's public did not see anything in their paintings that seemed abstract to them. The only thing that shocked them was the violence of this apparent fragmentation of reality. This violence made the exhibition of 1911 — which led to the spread of Cubism and included the works of many artists who had adopted the innovations introduced by their two precursors — a great success. A number of Italian artists like Boccioni, Russolo, Balla, and

PABLO PICASSO
Malaga, 1881 - Mougins, 1973
Woman's Head, 1907
(study for *Les Demoiselles d'Avignon*)
Oil on canvas
66 x 59
Purchased by the Musées Nationaux, 1965
AM 4320 P.

PABLO PICASSO
Malaga, 1881 - Mougins, 1973
Guitarist, 1909
Oil on canvas
100 x 73
Donated by M. and Mme André Lefèvre, 1952-1963
AM 3970 P.

Severini had formed a group around the poet Marinetti and had dubbed themselves the 'Futurists'. Their aim was to give expression to the speed, dynamism, and violence of the modern world. As a result, they inevitably found themselves in conflict with the Cubists, whose interest was focused on immobile objects and who accorded a different significance to painting. The Cubists' prime concern was the sensation of reality. And Braque was the first to incorporate real objects such as bits of newspaper, simulated wood, and chair caning into his paintings, giving the latter an illusion of space never previously seen.

Juan Gris preferred to effect the transposition of external subjects by means of painting rather than collage. Bright colours helped him to create a more ambiguous space. This interest in colour, initially excluded from Cubism, was what gave the work of Robert Delaunay and his wife, Sonia, its originality. The fragmented forms typical of Cubism allowed them to make free and lively use of large areas of flat colour. Colour harmonies were created on the basis of the complementary concordances already used in Impressionism. Their paintings no longer maintained anything but the most distant connection with the conventional representation of reality, of which just one or two traces persisted (cf. *A Window*).

From the point of view of chronology, the Cubist revolution began in painting, with Cubist sculpture only appearing somewhat later. The first and most important Cubist sculptors were Jacques Lipchitz, Raymond Duchamp-Villon, and Henri Laurens, and the Museum owns several important ensembles of these artists' work. Although all taking their inspiration from the dissolution of classical forms, each followed a different route — Lipchitz using static planes welded together, Duchamp-Villon seeking to recreate the mobility of the object fused with that of the eye, and Laurens — in his first works — introducing colour, which he used to modulate delicate structures. The influence exerted by Cubism on the production of younger artists lasted longer in sculpture than in painting. During the 1930s Julio González executed works in metal whose formal vocabulary appears radically new yet retains its proximity to basic Cubist language.

△

LUIGI RUSSOLO
Portogruaro, 1885 - Cerro, 1947
Dinamismo di un'Automobile, 1911
Oil on canvas
106 x 140
Donated by Mme Sonia Delaunay, 1949
AM 2917 P.

FERNAND LÉGER
Argentan, 1881 - Gif-sur-Yvette, 1955
The Roofs of Paris, 1912
Oil on canvas
90 x 64
Dation in payment for succession duties, 1985
AM 1985-400.

ROBERT DELAUNAY
Paris, 1885 - Montpellier, 1941
A Window, 1912/13
Oil on canvas
111 x 90
Purchased by the Musées Nationaux, 1950
AM 2975 P.

NATHALIA GONCHAROVA
Negaevo, 1881 - Paris, 1962
Woman with Hat, 1912
Oil on canvas
90 x 66
Donated by Jean Cassou, 1960
AM 3862 P.

◁

GEORGES BRAQUE
Argenteuil, 1882 - Paris, 1963
Woman with Guitar, 1913
Oil on canvas
130 x 73
Donated by Raoul La Roche, 1957
AM 3487 P.

SONIA DELAUNAY
Odessa, 1885 - Paris, 1979
Le Bal Bullier, 1913
Oil on canvas
97 x 390
Purchased by the State, 1954
AM 3307 P.

JUAN GRIS
Madrid, 1887 - Boulogne-sur-Seine, 1927
Breakfast, 1915
Oil and charcoal on canvas
92 x 73
Purchased by the Musées Nationaux, 1947
AM 2678 P.

GINO SEVERINI
Cortone, 1883 - Meudon, 1966
The Bear's Dance at the Moulin Rouge, 1913
Oil on canvas
100 x 73.5
Purchased by the State, 1950
AM 2992 P.

Francis Picabia
Paris, 1879 - Paris, 1953
Udnie, 1913
Oil on canvas
290 x 300
Purchased by the State, 1949
AM 2874 P.

RAYMOND DUCHAMP-VILLON
Damville, 1876 - Cannes, 1918
Cheval Majeur, 1914
Bronze
100 x 80 x 100
Purchased by the Musées Nationaux
(commission), 1955
AM 995 S.

26

The *Cheval Majeur* by Duchamp-Villon is the illustration of a superior being which inherited its elegance and permanence from the animal and its strength and beauty from the machine. The plastic language of Cubism turns this figure into an optimistic allegory of our modern world. The theme of the horse is one of the major themes in the history of sculpture while mechanical power is the revelation of the beginning of this century. Tradition merges with those elements which are considered to be the best of what human intelligence is capable of producing, and Cubism has the specific task of bringing these two opposites together, uniting past and future in one and the same formal entity.

Both lines and volumes are expressed with the same economy as that which rules the construction of machinery: all elements have a specific purpose and smoothly move around a central axis. As they move further away from the plinth, they rotate with growing intensity as if they are suddenly released by compressed air or a spring. The outside and the inside are just as visible as in a steam engine, the steel carapace of which reveals the main drive rods and wheels. Cubism which is very closely related to Futurism, clearly illustrates motion while underlining the static nature of a still-life.

The *Seated Woman* by Gaudier-Brzeska, who died before his time during the war, offers some similarities with the masterpiece by Duchamp-Villon. The disproportionate arms float in borad movements around the head and look as if they are locked into one another, resulting in an expression of uplift. The fluidity of this small sculpture allows our eyes to move unhindered from one area to another, from the full to the hollow parts which are placed in perfect equilibrium.

GAUDIER-BRZESKA
Saint-Jean-de-Braye, 1891 - Neuville-Saint-Vaast, 1915
Seated Woman, 1914
Marble
48 x 34.5 x 28
Donated by the Kettle's Yard Foundation, 1964
AM 1461 S.

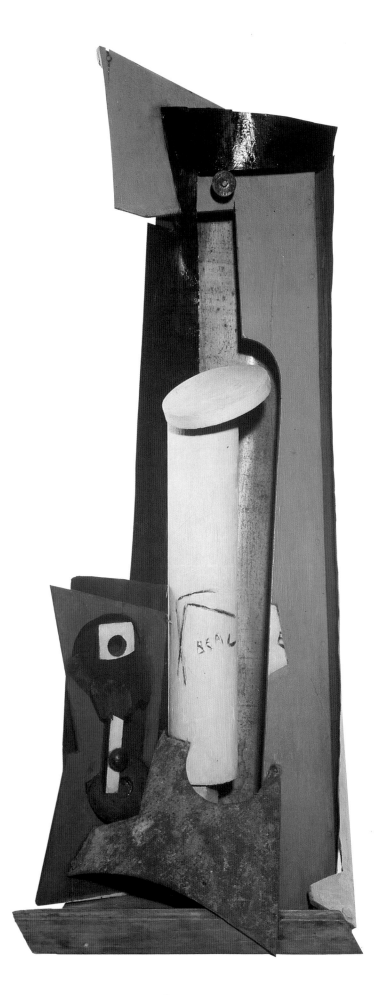

HENRI LAURENS
Paris, 1885 - Paris, 1954
The Bottle of Beaune, 1918
Wood and polychrome sheet steel
66.8 x 27 x 24
Purchased by CNAC GP, 1977
AM 1978-22.

ROBERT DELAUNAY
Paris, 1885 - Montpellier, 1941
Pig Farm, 1922
Oil on canvas
248 x 254
Donated by Mme Sonia Delaunay, 1955
AM 3384 P.

JACQUES LIPCHITZ
Druskieniki (USSR), 1891 - Capri, 1973
Study for *The Couple*, 1929
Plaster
38.5 x 76.2 x 38.5
Donated by the J. and Y. Lipchitz Foundation, 1976
AM 1976-839.

JULIO GONZÁLEZ
Barcelona, 1876 - Arceuil, 1942
Pointed Head, c. 1930
Bronze by means of *cire perdue*
31 x 17 x 11
Donated by Mme Roberta González, 1964
AM 1417 S.

Picasso

Of all the artists of the twentieth century, Picasso is the one who most effectively captured the diversity of the visible universe, whereas Matisse seemed more preoccupied with capturing harmony, its hidden order. Having invented Cubism and the *papier collé* with Braque, Picasso went on to incorporate these discoveries into a style of painting whose subjects, in the period just after the First World War, show a return to traditional vision. And yet he had distanced himself once and for all from illusionist representation. He was never again to paint as he had done at the age of twelve, when he could already 'draw like Raphael'. He explored the possibilities of figurative art and was to continue right into his last paintings to experiment with resemblance and to take every possible liberty with it, inventing not only his own formal vocabulary but also a still indeterminable number of pictorial languages. He took his inspiration from everything that was to hand, and used the universe of his private life as an inexhaustible source of ideas, all the while avoiding the trap of sentimentality. A number of works in the Museum's Picasso collection — expanded some years ago by the addition of the Louise and Michel Leiris Donation — were donated directly to the Museum by the artist.

Confidences is a large collage designed for a tapestry and depicting a *tête-à-tête* between two women. The woman on the right is speaking in a low voice, whilst the other woman, close up, kneeling in a chair, with her arms folded on the back, listens and reflects on what is being said. The listener's mouth is closed and she has her eyes shut, the better to drink in her friend's words. Her body seems to absorb everything: the armchair and the real wallpaper that Picasso has stuck on it. Only her head is visible, listening and meditating. The lips of the woman who is speaking are slightly open, her body is naked and diaphanous, elongated like an ivory chimney from which, as it were, invisible wisps of words emerge.

Aubade, another interior, is a large painting executed during the Occupation. The historical circumstances were probably not without their effect on the atmosphere evoked in this picture. The ideal image of an interior harmony is replaced by a vision of separate solitudes. The woman, lying naked on the bed, displays every facet of her anatomy to a man whose mind appears to be on other things. Distracted by his guitar, he sits stiffly, as if shocked by this body stretched out under a harsh electric light. The confrontational position of the two figures, set at right angles to each other, expresses the fundamental discord between them. From the somewhat inhospitable bed there extends an intimidating pattern of crenellations blocking the path of this over-romantic — or half-hearted — lover. The sharp lines dividing up the pictorial space give the painting the mournful look of a garret bedroom transformed into a cold-storage chamber.

PABLO PICASSO
Malaga, 1881 - Mougins, 1973
Confidences, 1943
Distemper and *papier collé* on canvas
194 × 170
Donated by Mme Paul Cuttoli, 1963-1969
AM 4210 P.

After the Second World War Picasso's 'styles' changed more rapidly, those of the later years often being violent and crude. *The Rape of the Sabine Women* brings together the two most violent themes in the history of art: the Sabine episode and the Massacre of the Innocents. The male figure, with his disproportionately large knife, recalls the figure in Poussin's painting, with the addition here of a kind of jubilant frenzy.

PABLO PICASSO
Malaga, 1881 - Mougins, 1973
The Muse, 1935
Oil on canvas
130 x 162
Donated by the artist, 1947
AM 2726 P.

PABLO PICASSO
Malaga, 1881 - Mougins, 1973
*The Rape of the Sabine
Women*, 1962
Oil on canvas
97 x 130
Donated by Daniel-Henry
Kahnweiler, 1964
AM 2428 P.

PABLO PICASSO
Malaga, 1881 - Mougins, 1973
Aubade, 1942
Oil on canvas
195 x 265
Donated by the artist, 1947
AM 2730 P.

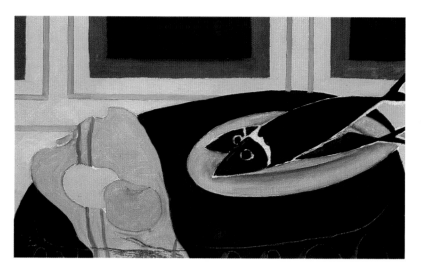

GEORGES BRAQUE
Argenteuil, 1882 - Paris, 1963
Black Fish, 1942
Oil on canvas
33 x 55
Donated by the artist, 1947
AM 2762 P.

Braque

The co-founder of Cubism, Braque was one of the protagonists of the modernist revolution. On resuming his artistic activity after being wounded in the First World War, he sought to reconcile Cubism and Classicism. This move won him increasing esteem amongst his contemporaries, and as a result he is excellently represented in the Museum's collection. The main features of Cubism which he retained were the expressive richness of discontinuous space, a restricted palette, and the use of relief in imitation of *papiers collés*. His favourite subject was the still-life, and it is no doubt within this genre that his best works are to be found. They possess a material and tactile quality that heightens the impression of the presence of the objects depicted. They demonstrate that one's vision of things involves not only 'purely visual' images but also physical touch and physical perception. His *Black Fish*, or the crucial *Studio* series — the last of which is owned by the Museum — stress the shifting quality of appearance: witness the fascinating image of fish placed like almond-shaped eyes on a silver dish. Braque applied the discoveries he made in relation to objects to his representation of animate beings. One of his last series of paintings was that of the birds, creatures more akin to one's picture of spirits than to animals.

GEORGES BRAQUE
Argenteuil, 1882 - Paris, 1963
The Bird and its Nest, 1955
Oil on canvas
130.5 x 173.5
Donated by Mme Georges Braque, 1963
AM 4307 P.

GEORGES BRAQUE
Argenteuil, 1882 - Paris, 1963
Studio IX, 1952-1956
Oil on canvas
146 x 146
Dation in payment for succession duties, 1982
AM 1982-99.

Léger

The Museum possesses the most complete collection — and one of exceptional quality — of the works of Fernand Léger. Léger, who is considered one of the major Cubist artists, worked in accordance with what he termed the 'law of contrasts', opposing flat and modelled surfaces, pure colours and grey tones, the rounded contours of the human body and geometric angles. His paintings are highly coloured (he was a regular visitor of Robert Delaunay's at La Ruche), and his admiration for Cézanne led him to adopt a rigorous approach to construction. He never abandoned figurative form. He was particularly sensitive to the 'superpoetic atmosphere of war', and the sight of a cannon breech lying open in the sun set him off on his 'mechanical period', which he envisaged as a homage to the plastic beauty of the machine and of the sleek mechanical objects of the modern world. From 1921 he participated, in his own individual way, in the 'call to order', seeking to define the human figure whilst treating it with the distance appropriate to a physical object. He invented his own particular physiognomy, consisting of highly articulated bodies and round faces on which the pronounced arch of the eyebrows is continued along the ridge of the nose,

forming a symmetrical sign over the mouth, always depicted closed. Yet the homogeneity of the faces and bodies does not preclude a gentle sensuality not possessed by physical objects. *Figures Reading* is one of the best examples. Two women, one lying down, the other standing, gaze out fixedly. Each holds a book, and this creates an atmosphere of deep concentration, further developed in the elaborate background. During the same period, in his *Composition with Four Hats*, Léger demonstrates his awareness of the visual discoveries of cinematography, of the effects of the juxtaposition of identical planes, of the spread of serialization in manufacture, and of the perception of the world that prevailed in the 1920s. These preoccupations do not, however, preclude his devoting himself, a little later, to the study of objects and details considered insignificant, and he is one of the first artists to realize the richness of such subjects. In his large-scale *Composition with Two Parrots* — which he regarded as one of his most successful works and donated to the Museum — the objects have an unreal presence that can be traced back directly to this research.

As in each major stage of his work, *The Black Divers* is based on an actual situation observed by Léger. In this instance the incident involved young dockers swimming in the harbour at Marseilles when Léger was about to leave for the United States, his home during the Second World War. Submerged bodies, shadows, and reflected sunlight intermingle. Colour and line now only bear a distant relation to the monumentality of his previous works. Both seem to have evolved towards a freer and more joyful mode of expression.

FERNAND LÉGER
Argentan, 1881 - Gif-sur-Yvette, 1955
Figures Reading, 1924
Oil on canvas
113.5 x 146
Bequeathed by Baroness Gourgaud, 1965
AM 3718 P.

FERNAND LÉGER
Argentan, 1881 - Gif-sur-Yvette, 1955
Composition with Four Hats, 1927
Oil on canvas
248 x 185.5
Dation in payment for succession duties, 1982
AM 1982-104.

FERNAND LÉGER
Argentan, 1881 - Gif-sur-Yvette, 1955
The Black Divers, 1944
Oil on canvas
189 x 217.5
Dation in payment for succession duties, 1982
AM 1982-102.

FERNAND LÉGER
Argentan, 1881 -
Gif-sur-Yvette, 1955
Composition with Two Parrots,
1935-1939
Oil on canvas
400 x 480
Donated by the artist, 1950
AM 3026 P.

Kandinsky

Following a series of donations and bequests — in particular the Nina Kandinsky Bequest —, the Museum has become one of the chief repositories of Kandinsky's work. His œuvre is well represented, since the collection includes not only a number of his earliest paintings, mid-way between Symbolism and Neo-Impressionism, but also works from the transitional phase between figurative and abstract art, as well as many of his later paintings, ranging right up to his last creative phase, the Parisian period. It was the discovery, at nightfall, of a painting lying on its side in his studio at Murnau that led Kandinsky to the revelation of a type of art without reference to the external world. He was the first to comprehend that it is perfectly possible for

WASSILY KANDINSKY
Moscow, 1866 - Neuilly-sur-Seine, 1944
Improvisation III, 1909
Oil on canvas. 94 x 130
Donated by Mme Kandinsky, 1976
AM 1976-850.

WASSILY KANDINSKY
Moscow, 1866 - Neuilly-sur-Seine, 1944
With Black Arch, 1912
Oil on canvas
189 x 198
Donated by Mme Kandinsky, 1976
AM 1976-852.

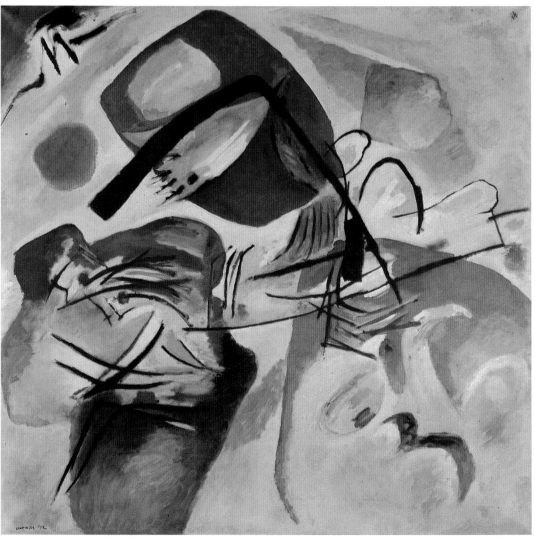

a painting to have no direct relation to the forms that exist in nature. With this discovery the artist gains a large measure of freedom, and the number of possible modes of expression becomes potentially infinite. In 1911, together with Franz Marc, Kandinsky founded the association *Der Blaue Reiter* (The Blue Rider) — a name taken from the almanach they edited. The group immediately had a great influence in Germany, where he was living, and in Russia, but its development was arrested by the war and by the Revolution of 1917. After the war the architect Walter Gropius invited Kandinsky to come and teach at the faculty of the Bauhaus, which he had recently founded. Kandinsky took an active part in the Bauhaus in Weimar (1922-1925) and then in Dessau (1915-1932), the last attempt to establish the school in Berlin being stifled by the Nazis on their advent to power. Nazi pressure forced Kandinsky to leave Germany for Paris, and he settled in Neuilly in 1939. Here he died, in 1944, shortly before his work achieved true recognition.

The use of titles that have no reference to the natural world is an attempt to convey the autonomy of the work in relation to external reality. *Improvisation III* shows a landscape in which a man on horseback is about to cross a bridge leading to a castle. The treatment of the subject gives the impression of an unreal vision, as in dreams or folktales. This world of the spirit, distinct from the concrete world, was no doubt a necessary transitional phase to an abstract vision of reality — a transition which in Kandinsky is much more effective than any rational deduction of forms. The great square painting *With Black Arch* became one of the artist's most famous canvases after his death. A central black line sets up a tension between the three swaying, gyrating masses. The static world has been replaced by a glimmering red universe. The multiple forms are arranged to recreate a universe capable of existing without any relation to the outside world. The precarious balance of Kandinsky's compositions seems to be the precondition for this self-generation of forms and colours, which, through dissonance, achieve a subtly perceptible balance. Over the last twenty years of his life, Kandinsky's forms evolved into a vocabulary. Geometric elements exist alongside particles that have a cellular appearance. In *Reciprocal Accord* Kandinsky pursues faithfully his research at a time when abstract art is generally abandoned.

WASSILY KANDINSKY
Moscow, 1866 -
Neuilly-sur-Seine, 1944
Reciprocal Accord, 1942
Oil and enamel paint on canvas
114 x 146
Donated by Mme Kandinsky, 1976
AM 1976-863.

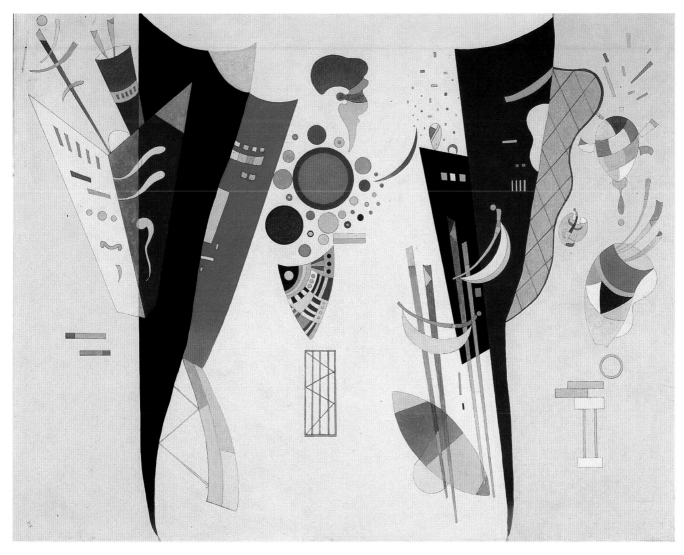

Klee

Klee took part in the activities of *Der Blaue Reiter*, along with Kandinsky, whose friend he was to remain. Having hesitated between the careers of musician and artist, he opted for the latter, though never forgetting that painting, like music, is capable of striking at the innermost feelings and of arousing the imagination. Klee's great skill is masked in the borrowed gaucherie of children's drawing. Besides teaching theory at the Bauhaus during the 1920s — his theories constitute one of the best approaches to art ever developed — Klee engaged in the creation of works that have an intimate appearance, but whose subjects and chosen titles reveal concerns of a universal order. As a result of careful observation of feelings and attitudes, of animals, and of plants, which he endowed with a fanciful appearance, the world which Klee creates reflects the variety of a naturalistic universe, a *comédie humaine*: a simple mark and colour applied to a piece of paper portray with great accuracy a situation, an expression, or more simply the morphology of a landscape or movement, each with their own particular quality of light and fluidity.

Klee spent the last years of his life to study the expressive possibilities of the line trying to illustrate as many things as possible with as few means as possible. In *Harbour with Sailing Ships* the boats are represented by only those indications which suffice to express their movement in the light reflected by the water. The dazzling sunshine is the effect of a subtle play with elementary colours producing an impression of profound silence, and a happiness which is so perfect that one can already feel the approach of a dramatic event: between the yachts and the boats tension appears to concentrate around the small floating jetty at the top of this delicate picture.

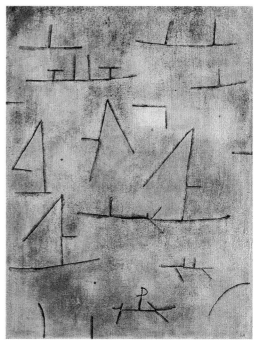

PAUL KLEE
Münchenbuchsee (Switzerland), 1879 - Locarno, 1940
Harbour with Sailing Ships, 1937
Oil on canvas
80 x 60.5
Donated by M. and Mme André Lefèvre, 1952
AM 3969 P.

PAUL KLEE
Münchenbuchsee (Switzerland), 1879 - Locarno, 1940
Rhythmic, 1930
Oil on jute canvas
69.6 x 50.5
Purchased by CNAC GP, 1984
AM 1984-356.

Brancusi

CONSTANTIN BRANCUSI
Pestisani (Rumania), 1876 - Paris, 1957
Sleeping Muse, 1910
Bronze with patina
16.5 x 26 x 18
Purchased by the Musées Nationaux, 1946
AM 818 S.

Constantin Brancusi invented a world in which the basic simplicity of the forms derives from the attentive observation of his models. After an academic artistic education in Rumania, he settled in Paris in 1904. The sculpture scene of the end of last century with its mythological themes expressive of pathos was considered to be the mainspring of plastic expression. Reacting against this, he embarked on a progressive purification of forms, seeking a compromise between the most faithful representation of the character of his model and a quintessential form. His models partly stemmed from the rich Rumanian folk art of his childhood. *Sleeping Muse* is an oval head lying on its side. It is the whole object that is lying — no neck, no shoulders, no plinth — as if the material itself — bronze, stone or plaster — (the Museum possesses several versions of it) was resting and dreaming. Only just visible are the double arches of the eyebrows, the bone of the nose, the asymmetric slit of the mouth and the fine shell of the ear. Brancusi's familiarity with the world of natural forms enables the Muse to achieve the original form

Abstraction Between the Wars

THEO VAN DOESBURG
Utrecht, 1883 - Davos, 1931
Composition, 1920
Oil on canvas
130 x 80.5
Purchased by the Musées Nationaux, 1964
AM 4281 P.

The conflict between figurative and abstract art has the advantage of allowing a distinction which in practice produces numerous contradictions and problems. Take a picture by Mondrian for example. Is it really abstract, isn't it just a question of orthogonal lines and coloured rectangles and doesn't it represent anything? Arp was of the opinion that the shapes man produces belong to nature and cannot be divorced from her — they spring directly from her as fruit from a tree. Hence the term 'Concrete Art', which many artists preferred to abstract art, refusing to appear to be clothing ideas in a specific form. His humour had led him in the direction of Dada and he used it when his development inclined towards a mood in which poetry was becoming more and more prevalent. His reliefs in coloured wood and his sculptures show that lines and colours which do not evoke familiar things can look playful or gay and can express all sorts of emotions without using conventional human features. The plastic world of his wife, Sophie Taeuber-Arp, is more abstract, and the elements which make up her pictures are articulated more mechanically. They emanate a subtle, joyful atmosphere.

Van Doesburg constructs his pictures in the spirit of an architect or town-planner. With Mondrian he founded the *De Stijl* group, whose ideas he actively spread (Neo-Plasticism). Under the influence of Cubism, Mondrian progressively transformed his Fauve landscapes of 1906 into compositions with orthogonal lines on a white ground and squares of pure colours. Up to the early 1940s, the compositions were to become broader and the lines were to change into black bars criss-crossing to form a grid. He was a theoretician as well and in the period following the First World War, had published his conception of art defined as Neo-Plasticism. His vision was an art capable of impinging on the real by reflecting an intense image on it, harmoniously balanced like the geometrical tensions which exist in the universe. *Composition II* is the first of the two works by this painter which have become part of the collection. It was executed at the end of his stay in Paris which lasted from 1919 to 1938. He was the co-founder in 1929 of the group *Cercle et Carré*, which brought together, among others, Michel Seuphor, Torres-García, Baumeister, Kandinsky, Arp, Pevsner, Vantongerloo and Schwitters. Because of the uncertain pre-war climate, he left Paris for London and later New York. His later works are more dynamic and only the lines are coloured.

The climate of the Revolution gave Russian artists the feeling of a new reality which they felt in duty bound to represent in their art. Encouraged by the social upheaval which was brewing, the artists applied the aesthetic innovations of Fauvism and Cubism which they had been the first to see in some Moscow collections. Their aim was to use their work effectively to promote the objectives of the Revolution. *Black Cross* by Kasimir Malevich is one of those works of great significance for this brief period of hope. As an example of Suprematism, it confers on the new political era 'the supremacy of pure feeling in creative art'. Thus it uses a language established on permutations of the basic forms of circle and square; a cross is the result of two halves

of a square pivoting on each other. Malevich fulfill-
ed an important official function during the first
stage of the Revolution, a role he was to lose almost
as quickly as his illusions. His plans for architecture
in plaster were Utopian schemes. Very soon he
developed the discoveries of Cubism to the point of
abstraction, to the virtually total absence of colours
and shapes with the *Black Square* and the *White
Square*. He applied the formal economy of Suprematism (the tensions between colours values and volume were decisive) to a form of painting which had
again become figurative, thus achieving his final
and strangest masterpieces. Malevich's contemporaries were the artists of the Constructivist movement in Russia in the years between 1920 and 1927:
Gabo, El Lissitzky, Rodchenko, Tatlin and Pevsner. They sought a neutrality of expression and a
new perception of space by means of a mode of
composition which drew its inspiration from architecture. Pevsner avoided volume in favour of transparency and movement.

ANTOINE PEVSNER
Orel (USSR), 1886 - Paris, 1962
Mask, 1923
Celluloid and metal
33 x 20 x 20
Purchased by the State, 1974
AM 1974-24.

JEAN ARP
Strasbourg, 1886 - Locarno, 1966
Landscape Head, 1924-1926
Oil-painted wood
58 x 40.5 x 4.5
Purchased by CNAC GP, 1985
AM 1985-39.

LASZLO MOHOLY-NAGY
Bacsbarsod (Hungary), 1895 - Chicago, 1946
Composition A XX, 1924
Oil on canvas
135.5 x 115
Donated by the Friends of the MNAM
AM 4025 P.

PIET MONDRIAN
Amersfoort (Holland), 1872 - New York, 1944
Composition II, 1937
Oil on canvas
75 x 60.5
Purchased by the Musées Nationaux, 1975
AM 1975-53.

PIET MONDRIAN
Amersfoort (Holland), 1872 - New York, 1944
New York City I, 1942
Oil on canvas
119.3 x 114.2
Purchased by CNAC GP, 1984

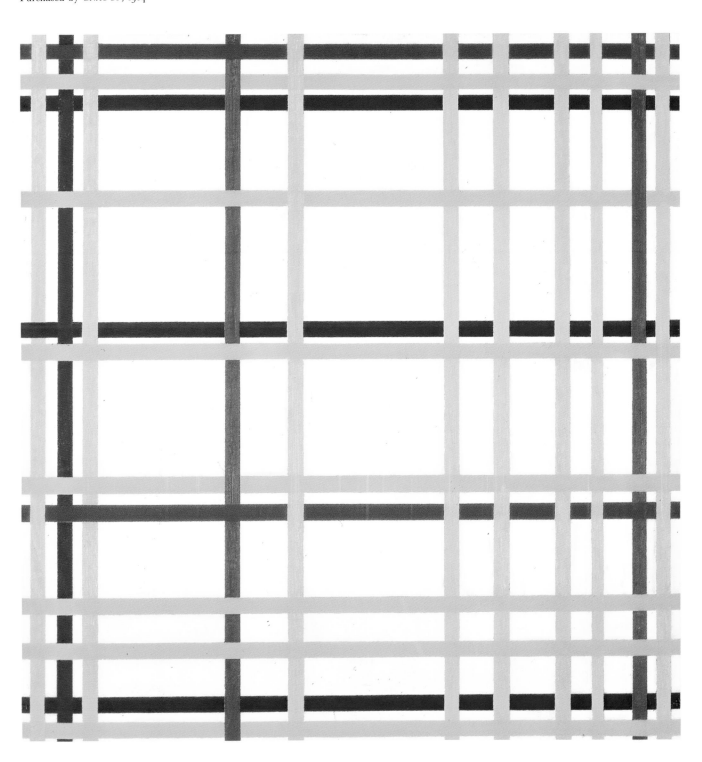

KASIMIR MALEVICH
Kiev, 1878 - Leningrad, 1935
Black Cross, 1915
Oil on canvas
80 x 79.5
Donated by the Scaler Foundation and Beaubourg
Foundation, 1979
AM 1980-1.

KASIMIR MALEVICH
Kiev, 1878 - Leningrad, 1935
Man Running, 1933/34
Oil on canvas
79 x 65
Anonymous gift, 1978
AM 1978-630.

Realism Between the Wars

In France military victory revived the belief in a strong and authoritative artistic tradition, the product of a national spirit unique in the world. Such ideas commanded fairly widespread respect, supported as they were by the press and by the main literary movements, with the exception of the currents from which Surrealism and abstraction were to spring. The innovations made in the name of Cubism were seen as excesses, and attempts were made to bring them into line with tradition. André Derain had distanced himself from Cubism even before the First World War. In the *Portrait of Itturino*, the human figure, as in Modigliani, has the same plasticity as an object. On his demobilization he was increasingly to adopt a middle way, trying to express the tensions of the modern world in a classical form, in the expression on a woman's face or in oranges casually placed on a table. Later this plasticity was to be absorbed by the light and atmosphere of the scene or the model. He shared the aims of a sculptor like Despiau but was far removed from the dream world of Marc Chagall. The *Double-portrait with Glass of Wine* represents the artist and his young wife in passionate levitation above a fairy scene in his native Russia. Their faces counteract the effect of giddiness by expressing their human intimacy.

The portrait of *The Journalist Sylvia von Harden* by Otto Dix is unequivocally more akin to the fierceness of Dada than to the concern for harmony and inwardness existing at the same time in France and Italy. This shapeless body, scarcely contained in a tube dress with large squares, shows two gigantic hands and the livid face of a cocaine addict. Fixing a monocle in her eye after expunging all traces of her sensuality, she freely parades her cigarette case. This is a far cry from the women of Cranach, whose composition and technique Dix takes up and puts to his own contrary uses. In comparison with the present-day hell, in which the coldness of the red and pink marble creates an atmosphere like a butcher's back shop, the German Renaissance looks like a lost paradise. Max Beckmann who was likewise associated with the *Neue Sachlichkeit* (New Objectivity) and its cruelties, developed in the course of the 1920s towards a technically less harsh realism. In *The Small Fish*, the fisherman's offering is a thinly veiled sexual overture. This game between men and women, accomplices in their feigning of surprise and innocence, adds to the strictnesss of the composition the piquancy of a simple and emotive subject.

Soutine's *Groom* comes across like a laboratory guinea-pig. The maximum opening of the limbs and the blood-red colour of the uniform contrast with the indifferent, slightly distressed look, a sign that his rather demeaning occupation affects him only superficially. He dances attendance, he hustles and bustles, but keeps himself to himself. His true life is elsewhere. The gold buttons are like carefully placed surgical stitches. They bring out the cynicism, the emptiness of all feeling, conferring on this portrait of a slave the sovereignty of a court portrait.

MARC CHAGALL ▷
Vitebsk (USSR), 1887 - Saint-Paul-de-Vence, 1985
Double-portrait with Glass of Wine, 1917/18
Oil on canvas
235 x 137
Donated by the artist, 1949
AM 2774 P.

AMEDEO MODIGLIANI
Leghorn, 1884 - Paris, 1920
Woman's Head, 1912
Stone
58 x 12 x 16
Purchased by the Musées Nationaux, 1949
AM 876 S.

OTTO DIX   ▷
Untermhaus, 1891 - Singen, 1969
The Journalist Sylvia von Harden, 1926
Oil and tempera on wood
121 x 89
Purchased by the Musées Nationaux, 1961
AM 3899 P.

RAOUL DUFY
Le Havre, 1877 - Forcalquier, 1955
Women Bathing in the Open Sea with Shells,
c. 1925-1927
Oil on canvas
116 x 89
Bequeathed by Mme Dufy, 1963
AM 4131 P.

ALBERT MARQUET
Bordeaux, 1875 - Paris, 1947
Blonde Woman, 1919
Oil on canvas
98.5 x 98.5
Donated by Olivier Senn, 1939
AM 2229 P.

JEAN FAUTRIER
Paris, 1898 - Châtenay-Malabry, 1964
The Flayed Wild Boar, 1927
Oil on canvas
163 x 131
Purchased by the State, 1937
AM 2179 P.

MARC CHAGALL
Vitebsk (USSR), 1887 - Saint-Paul-de-Vence, 1985
Angel holding a Palette, 1927-1936
Oil on linen canvas (second state)
131.5 x 89.7
Dation in payment for succession duties, 1988
AM 1988-65.

CHAÏM SOUTINE
Smilovichi (USSR), 1893 - Paris, 1943
The Groom, 1928
Oil on canvas
98 x 80.5
Matsukata sequestration
AM 3611 P.

ANDRÉ DERAIN
Chatou, 1880 - Garches, 1954
Still-life with Oranges, 1931
Oil on canvas
89 x 117
Purchased by the State, 1936
AM 2095 bis P.

MAX BECKMANN
Leipzig, 1884 - New York, 1950
The Small Fish, 1933
Oil on canvas
135 x 115
Purchased by the State, 1933
JP 679 P.

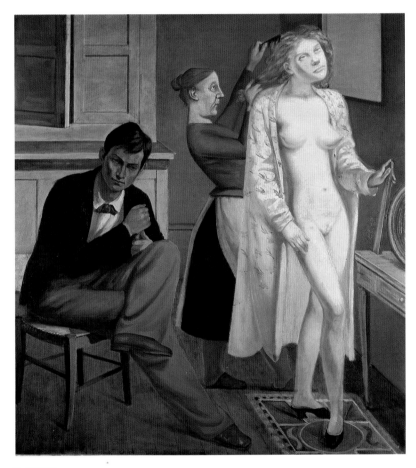

Charles Despiau
Mont-de-Marsan, 1874 - Paris, 1946
Study of a Face, c. 1934
Terre grise
22 x 13 x 10
Bequeathed by Mme Despiau, 1960
AM 1290 S.

Balthus
Paris, 1908
Cathy's Toilette, 1933
Oil on canvas
165 x 150
Purchased by CNAC GP
AM 1977-196.

Dada and Surrealism

Dada sprang from disgust with everything, in Zurich in 1916, right in the middle of the war, during a meeting of friends in a night club. The word is said to have been coined by the poet Tristan Tzara on opening a dictionary at random. The Dada philosophy and movement have no features. They have the energy of a passionate anarchy with which there is no coming to grips, which stems from the feeling of life dwindling and of the need for vital renewal. In France the artists and writers who subscribed to it were contemptuous of artistic and literary idolatry, tolerating only the schoolboy pranks of someone like Alfred Jarry, wildly mocking everything beautiful and serious and ending up by mocking Dada itself. Provocative statements and performances were the basic content of their artistic activities of which few works remain. Their state of mind fated them to compete with masterpieces in the way that children ape adults, knowing that the grimaces have far greater power than the studied certainties. After the armistice Dada spread all through the western world and enjoyed a brief but intensive existence in Berlin. With the military defeat came a sense that reality had melted away. The political context is particularly apparent in the works of George Grosz and Raoul Hausmann and even more in those of Otto Dix. It was against the background of a tragically abortive revolution that Raoul Hausmann produced the *Mechanical Head*, a polished wooden head with empty eyes and a set expression, equipped with small instruments for measuring, filing and writing, with a purse and a folding drinking-cup. These are the trappings of the thoughts and predilections of modern man. This montage which could be nothing other than an act of defiance against the bourgeoisie, goes far beyond political caricature.

The collection of Dadaist works in the Museum has just been complemented by the donation of *Bündel eines Da*, by Jean Arp who was with Tzara in 1916 when the movement was born. Made up of scraps, this collage of pieces of driftwood, this travelling case is akin to the works of his friend Kurt Schwitters who declared 'The world's detritus shall be my art', and used anything that had been thrown away. The materials have a coarse appearance which accords ill with the sensitivity that arranged them on this unusable board. But the unpleasantness of the materials is eclipsed by the interplay and quality of the colours and shapes. This freedom of action and thought was to have a revival even more striking than its first incarnation starting in the early 1960s when it was to Dada that many artists turned in their opposition to prevailing taste. And it was the rediscovery of this mood that prompted museums to seek out Dadaist works. But the Dadaist family tree had two ancestors, namely Marcel Duchamp and Francis Picabia. These artists challenged the stilted nature of art and after some early endeavours in Neo-Impressionist and Cubist vein they each embarked separately on a style which strove to discourage any cult that might crystallise around it. They made mobility of ideas their watchword.

Picabia states: 'If you want to have ideas of your own, change them like your shirts.' In the course of an Atlantic crossing the movements of a girl dancing on the bridge of the steamer were the inspiration for *Udnie*. The words in the picture stamp the work just as much as formal elements. After the war, when he was with Duchamp in the midst of the Parisian Dadaist activities, he asked his friends to append their signatures and write their comments on a picture which he painted to celebrate his recovery, following the custom of signing the plaster of a friend with a broken leg. He suffered from glaucoma and had been treated with cacodylate. He painted the saved eye surmounted with the inscription L'OEIL CACODYLATE. His criticism of painting did not confine itself simply to the mockery of technical procedures; he opposed all conventions. In *The Sphinx* traditional hierarchical arrangement of figure and background in the picture is turned topsy-turvy so that the silhouettes of the figures and objects are superposed on each other by means of transparency. It would not be long before he would do the same with the conventions of modern painting and would maintain an ironic distance.

Today Marcel Duchamp is a legendary figure in modern art. Although the actual number of his works is not very great, each one presents itself to contemporary exegesis with the insistence of an enigma. He is known especially for the invention of what he called the 'ready-made'. In 1912 he selected for display as a work of art a bicycle wheel mounted on a stool. He was to do the same thing several times, sometimes taking some manufactured object which he selected for presentation after he had signed it. The individual choice is more important here than the style or process and it is above all the selection that determines the style. Most of the ready-mades were lost and belatedly re-made by Duchamp. The Museum has a very representative set of them, complemented by a few unique pieces such as *George Washington*, a cover design for *Life*, in which the lost profile of the American president merges into the map of the United States made of gauze studded with thirteen stars.

At the beginning of the 1920s, Dada in France was to develop into Surrealism. This was a word of Appollinaire's taken up by André Breton who had associated with the poet before his death. In 1924 Breton published the *Premier Manifeste de Surréalisme* which enabled him to state his aesthetic position and to distance himself from Dada, whose attitude he criticized because in his view it had become bound by rules. As a young writer, Breton built up around him what has been called an 'aristocratie du miracle', in which each member, whether artist, writer or poet, would enjoy a state of total leisure which would enable him to have an uninterrupted series of successes in his early career. Surrealism proposed making life more intense by connecting it with dreams, wanton love and the unlimited exercise of freedom. Art was accepted to the extent that it

Francis Picabia
Paris, 1879 - Paris, 1953
L'OEil Cacodylate, 1921
Oil on canvas and collage of photos, postcards, papers
148.6 x 117.4
Purchased by the State, 1967
AM 4408 P.

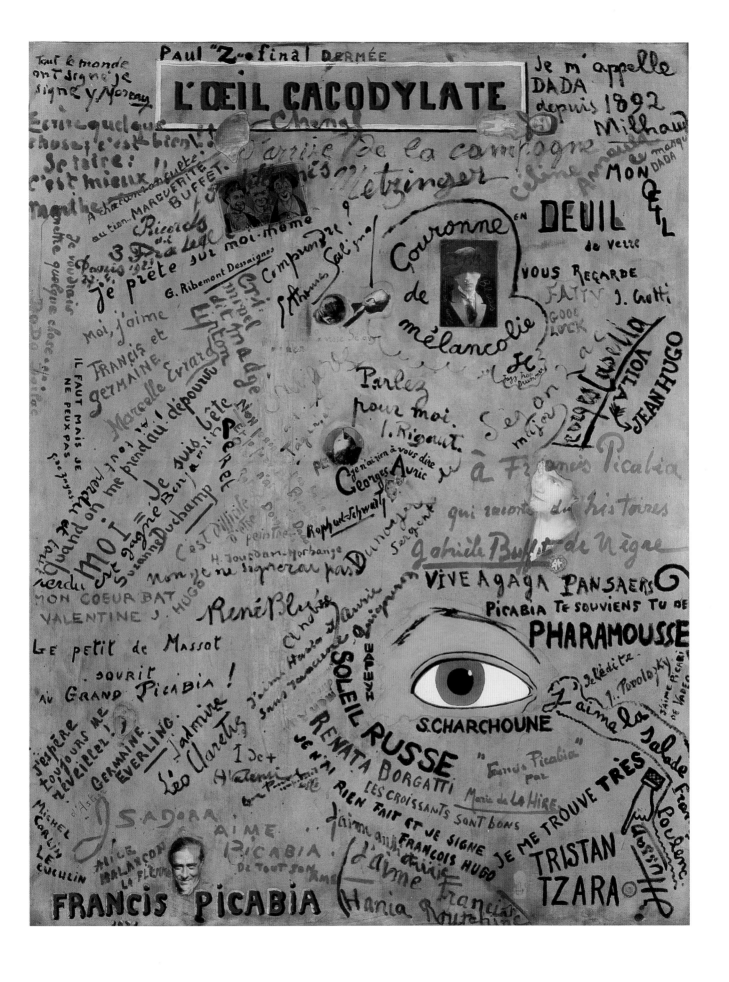

permitted a distortion in the normal perception of life. Surrealistic works must act like plummets cast in an intense exploration of freedom. Breton succeeded in giving the dynamic thrust of Dada a form and an objective. He defined it as 'a psychic automatism by which it is intended to express... the true function of thought'. Surrealism invades an area occupied hitherto only by the fringes of artistic creation. Automatism may be regarded as a weapon against the alleged sophisticated greatness of the French mind and of the realism which was developing at the same period, and aiming at something more true than external reality. The states of mind preceding sleep and the creations of dreams were regarded as the models for this new art. Breton who was a painting enthusiast with outstanding connoisseurship, succeeded, by organizing frequent meetings and trips, in extending the movement far beyond national frontiers. He realized that painting was probably the art closest to Surrealism by reason of its connection with the brain, since it functioned without consciousness necessarily being involved.

The Museum's Surrealist collection was largely built up in the course of the last fifteen years and consists at present of a set of works of the first rank. In it the works of Max Ernst have pride of place. *Ubu Imperator* depicts the head, hesitant and pon-

derous, of Alfred Jarry's famous character. Jarry was one of the rare writers, along with Lautréamont and Sade, whom the Surrealists admired unreservedly. Ernst stated that he was present as a spectator at the creation of his pictures, in which forms and colours are connected in unexpected ways. By rubbing his pencil on a canvas or a sheet of paper laid on an object he causes shapes to appear which suggest a different order of life from the one that is familiar to us. *Jardin Gobe-Avion* is one of the best products of this individual technique in which chance and freakishness are dominant. Salvador Dali used more academic procedures, harnessed to an unusual imagination fed on obsessions, dreams and stockpiled fancies. *Partial Hallucination, Six Images of Lenin on a Piano* is supposed to depict a nocturnal dream.

René Magritte who played only a marginal role in the events organized by the movement in Paris is one of its most influential painters. While painting only familiar objects in unexpected situations, he achieves the maximum sense of disorientation. *The Double Secret* shows the face of a young woman horrifyingly repeated against the background of a calm sea. The face beside a window frame is mutilated by a gaping wound containing bells which are typical of Magritte. This schizo-

MARCEL DUCHAMP
Blanville, 1887 - Paris, 1968
Bicycle Wheel, 1913-1964
Ready-made: assemblage of bicycle wheel on stool
126.5 x 31.5 x 63.5
Purchased by CNAC GP, 1986
AM 1986-286.

MARCEL DUCHAMP
Blanville, 1887 - Paris, 1968
Hat Rack, 1917-1964
Ready-made: hat rack in wood
27 x 44.5
Purchased by CNAC GP, 1986
AM 1986-293.

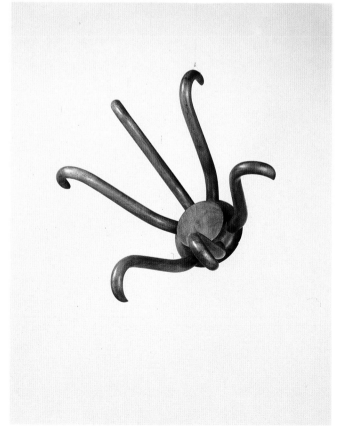

Jean Arp
Strasbourg, 1886 - Locarno, 1966
Bündel eines Da, 1920/21
Assemblage: driftwood nailed to partially painted wood
38.7 x 27 x 4.5
Donated by M. and Mme Christophe Tzara, 1989
AM 1989-195.

GIORGIO DE CHIRICO ▷ ▷
Volos (Greece), 1888 - Rome, 1978
Premonitory Portrait of Guillaume Apollinaire, 1914
Oil on canvas
81.5 x 65
Purchased by the Musées Nationaux, 1975
AM 1975-52.

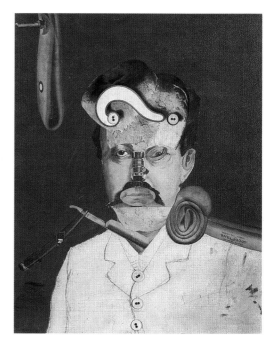

SOPHIE TAEUBER-ARP
Davos, 1889 - Zurich, 1943
Dada Head, *c*. 1918/19
Painted wood
34 x 20 x 20
Donated by Mme Arp, 1967
AM 1692 S.

GEORGE GROSZ
Berlin, 1893 - Berlin, 1959
Remember Uncle August the Unhappy Inventor, 1919
Oil, pencil, paper glued to canvas, 5 buttons incorporated
49 x 39.5
Purchased by CNAC GP, 1977
AM 1977-562.

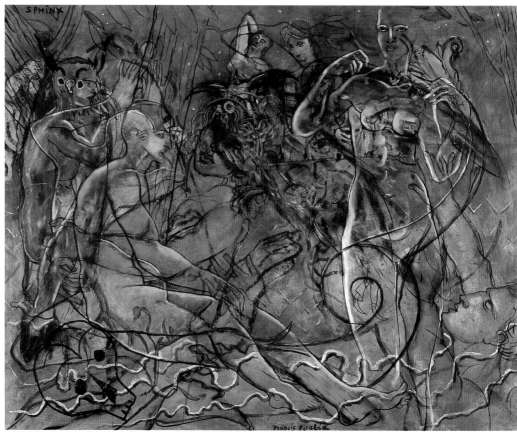

FRANCIS PICABIA
Paris, 1879 - Paris, 1953
The Sphinx, 1929
Oil on canvas
131 x 163
Purchased by the State, 1933
JP 668 P.

phrenic situation is disturbing in its symmetry. The calm beauty of the face is the reflection of something whose horror is at once visible and uncertain. The academic treatment in Magritte's paintings gives these pictures the disturbing appearance of a blatant yet unproved lie. What is being said is presented with so much care that it may well be false, excessive and cruel, but for all that may contain an element of truth.

In the course of the 1930s and in the period immediately following the Second World War, Surrealism developed in a direction in which automatism is most often dominant. Younger artists allied themselves to the movement, seeking in it an expression of spontaneity, of unfamiliar and totally autonomous pictorial language. It often seems that the majority of those who painted the content of dreams in *trompe-l'œil* gradually seemed to be running out of subjects. The pictures of Yves Tanguy represent a desert-like world of submarine, subterranean or lunar scenes. The shadows are given a more real presence than the objects. In the course of this second phase of Surrealism, signs are given more

prominence. André Masson tries to rediscover the spontaneity of drawing by incorporating sand into his pictures, stuck on at random. Roberto Matta piles up signs in which images emerge as in a carpet, images which constitute a universe inhabited by creatures in human guise and endowed with human obsessions.

A certain vocabulary made up of rounded or oval shapes, imperceptible lines and precarious balances, as well as an almost parallel development, and above all a similar sense of humour links the works of Joan Miró with those of Alexander Calder. *The Siesta* is clearly quite a different subject from *Josephine Baker I*, but in the bluish air of the picture there appear (or disappear) a few half-real elements which represent the animation of a world which is no less coherent, no less mysterious in its movements, and no less attractive than the body of the black woman dancer, which it is difficult to imagine in wrought iron. Later, apparently under the influence of Mondrian, Calder's mobiles were to lose something of their sensuality but would retain their enigmatic character. Thus *Constellation* is an apparently static stellar map.

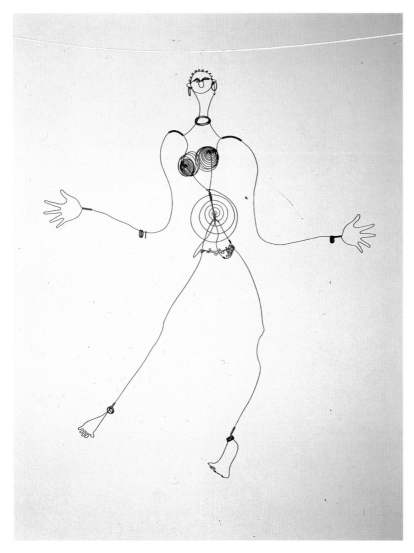

MAX ERNST
Brühl (West-Germany), 1891 - Paris, 1976
Ubu Imperator, 1923
Oil on canvas
81 x 65
Donated by the Fondation pour la Recherche
Médicale, 1984
AM 1984-281.

ALEXANDER CALDER
Philadelphia, 1898 - New York, 1976
Josephine Baker I, 1926
Wire
101 x 95 x 25
Donated by the artist, 1966
AM 1518 S.

66

JOAN MIRÓ
Barcelona, 1893 - Palma de Mallorca, 1983
The Siesta, 1925
Oil on canvas
113 x 146
Purchased by CNAC GP, 1977
AM 1977-203.

MAN RAY
Philadelphia, 1890 - Paris, 1976
One Night at Saint-Jean-de-Luz, 1929
Oil on canvas
73 x 54
Deposited by the State, 1967
AM 4407 P.

René Magritte
Lessines, 1898 - Brussels, 1967
The Double Secret, 1927
Oil on canvas
114 x 162
Purchased by CNAC GP, 1979
AM 1980-2.

Yves Tanguy
Paris, 1900 - Woodbury (USA), 1955
A quatre heures d'Été, l'Espoir, 1929
Oil on canvas
129.5 x 97
Purchased by CNAC GP, 1978
AM 1978-321.

SALVADOR DALI
Figueras (Spain), 1904 - Figueras, 1989
Partial Hallucination. Six Images of Lenin on a Piano, 1931
Oil on canvas
114 x 146
Purchased by the State, 1938
AM 2909 P.

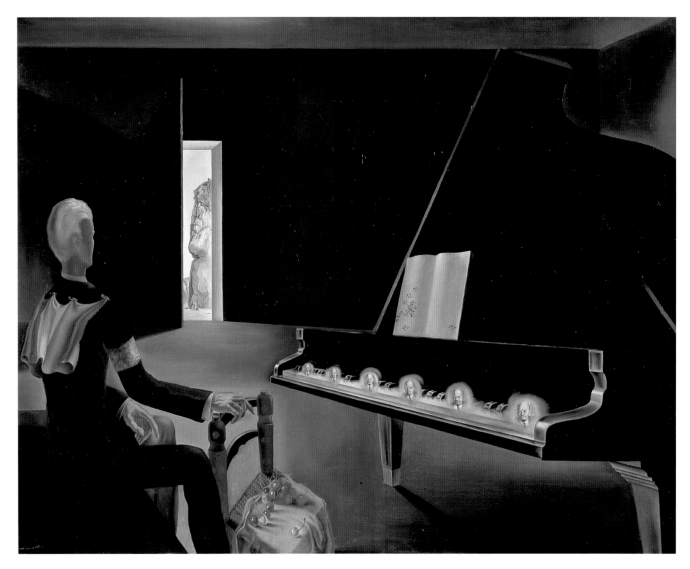

MAX ERNST
Brühl (West-Germany), 1891 - Paris, 1976
Jardin Gobe-Avion, 1935
Oil on canvas
54 × 74
Dation in payment for succession duties, 1982
AM 1982-188.

RENÉ MAGRITTE
Lessines, 1898 - Brussels, 1967
The Red Model, 1935
Oil on canvas glued to cardboard
56 × 46
Purchased by the Musées Nationaux, 1975
AM 1975-216.

JOAN MIRÓ
Barcelona, 1893 - Palma de Mallorca, 1983
Objet du Couchant, 1935/36
Assemblage: painted wood, metal and string
68 x 44 x 26
Purchased by the Musées Nationaux, 1975
AM 1975-56.

VICTOR BRAUNER
Piatra Neamtz (Rumania), 1903 - Paris, 1966
Wolf-Table, 1939-1947
Wood and fragments of stuffed fox
54 x 57 x 28.5
Donated by Mme Brauner, 1974
AM 1974-27.

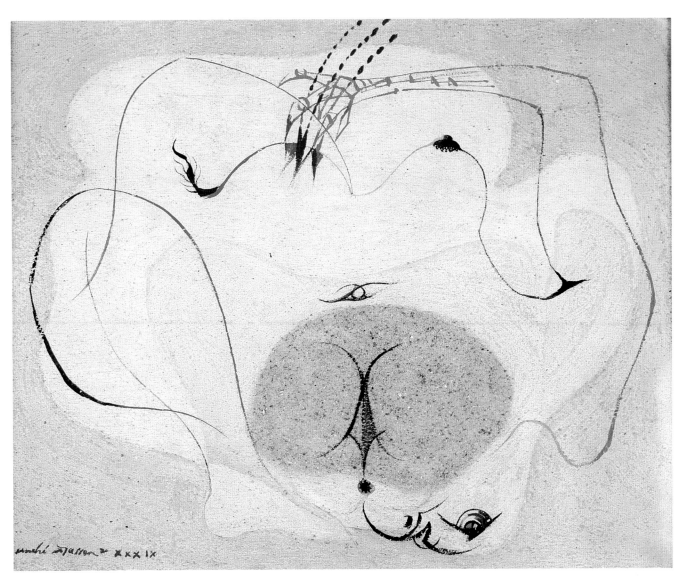

ANDRÉ MASSON
Balagny, 1896 - Paris, 1987
The Earth, 1939
Sand and oil on plywood
43 x 53
Donated by Mme Masson, 1965
AM 4318 P.

MARCEL DUCHAMP
Blanville, 1887 - Paris, 1968
George Washington, 1943
Assemblage: dyed gauze, cotton wool,
cut-up gouache paper on wood
54.8 x 42.7 x 7
Purchased by CNAC GP, 1987
AM 1987-632.

ROBERTO MATTA
Santiago de Chile, 1911
Xpace and the Ego, 1945
Oil on canvas
202.2 x 457.2
Purchased by CNAC GP, 1983
AM 1983-94.

ALEXANDER CALDER
Philadelphia, 1898 - New York, 1976
Constellation, 1943
Painted wood and wire
61 x 72 x 53
Donated by the artist, 1966
AM 1530 S.

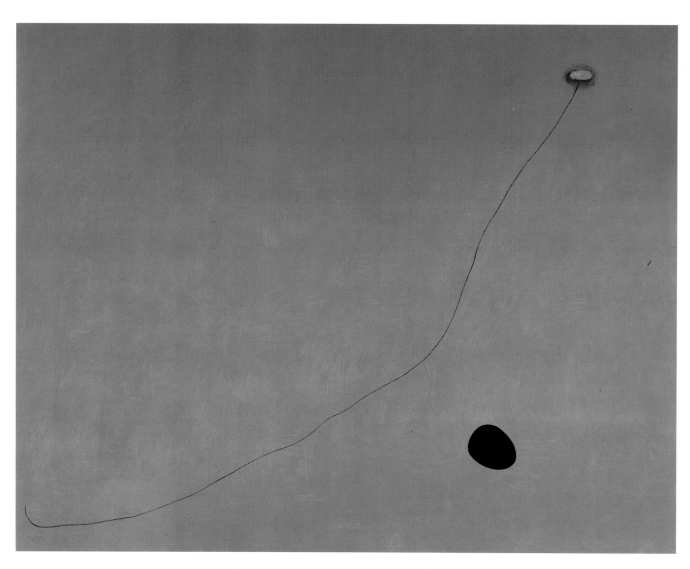

JOAN MIRÓ
Barcelona, 1893 - Palma de Mallorca, 1983
Blue III, 1961
Oil on canvas
268 x 349
Purchased by CNAC GP 1988
AM 1988-569.

Giacometti

Alberto Giacometti is an artist whose development follows faithfully, although at some distance, the broad artistic currents in sculpture, of which he is one of the most inventive exponents. After his training (he sculpted portraits of members of his family at the age of thirteen), his work passes imperceptibly from Cubism to Surrealism, to those spindly static figures which have made him famous. They express that attention which the post-war period uneasily paid to the inner life of human beings. None the less, in spite of differences in style, the subject is the human body in a situation of extreme tension. The works of the Surrealist period have, moreover, not much in common with dream fantasy. His bodies and heads made of a rectangular strip with slightly convex surfaces and marked with slight hollows, represent very well a body or a face with signs adapted from primitive sculpture. He succeeds in re-creating half visual, half tactile images of a body or face. Around 1930 his compact sculptures are emptied of their substance and become open structures. Inside the 'cages' more or less figurative elements operate like actors attacking or being attacked. Their proportions change according as they appear at one and the same time more vulnerable and more dangerous and their presence is thereby heightened. *Point to the Eye* is an open cage whose limits are suggested by the format of the plinth. A human figure is identifiable by its little thoracic cage surmounted by a head in which the eye sockets are the origin (or the target) of a long tapering shape whose point grazes them.

Giacometti was at last recognized soon after the war partly thanks to the study of him by Jean-Paul Sartre and Jean Genet. The figures he models, draws and paints, have incorporated the violence of the previous works and the impression of presence that they give is more intense. They show the essence of the human: the upright position and man's consciousness of his isolation.

ALBERTO GIACOMETTI
Borgonovo ob Stampa, 1901 - Coire, 1966
Point to the Eye, 1932
Wood and iron
12.5 x 53.2 x 29.5
Purchased by CNAC GP, 1981
AM 1981-251.

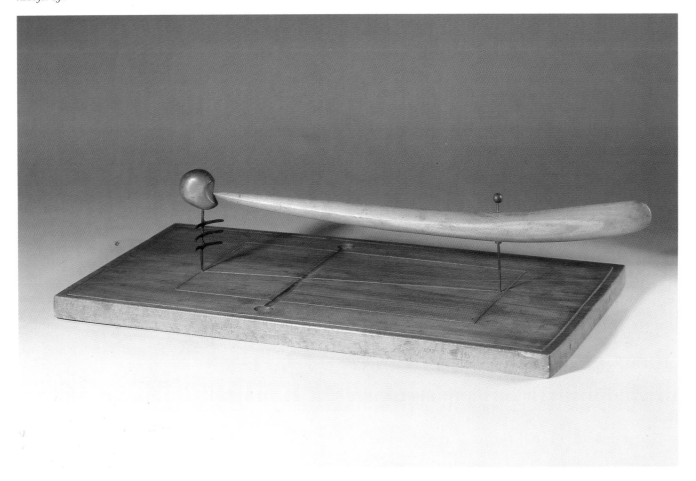

ALBERTO GIACOMETTI
Borgonovo ob Stampa, 1901 - Coire, 1966
Woman, 1927
Original plaster
55.3 x 33.1 x 7.8
Purchased by CNAC GP with the assistance
of the Scaler Foundation, 1982
AM 1982-13.

ALBERTO GIACOMETTI
Borgonovo ob Stampa, 1901 - Coire, 1966
Seated Woman, 1956
Bronze
77.5 x 14.5 x 19.5
Donated by Aimé Maeght, 1977
AM 1977-217.

ALBERTO GIACOMETTI
Borgonovo ob Stampa, 1901 - Coire, 1966
Portrait of Jean Genet, 1955
Oil on canvas
73 x 60
Purchased by CNAC GP, 1980
AM 1980-35.

The Post-War Period

Rejecting the external world and propelled by an inner need — the main features retained from Surrealism — many artists embarked on the path of non-geometric abstraction. The subject was worked out on the canvas and the meaning did not emerge until the colours and lines had been put in place. The brushstroke translated the emotion they hoped to transmit without the intermediary of form which was felt to be an obstacle to the pure expression of emotion. In France the search for authentic individual experience meant that this post-war period was one rich in experiment. The essential aesthetic focus for more than fifteen years would now be in the abstract sphere of the undefined image. Fautrier, who exhibited in the 'Salon des Realités Nouvelles' in 1946, shows mangled bodies which were so unrecognizable that they were thought to be abstract. Nicolas de Staël does not seem to take account of the split between abstract and figurative art. The lightness and balance of the forms contrast with the heavy treatment of the paint. He was to move away from half-tone colours in favour of the brighter pictures which preceded his suicide. There was a parallel development of abstract currents, stigmatized by their differences. It seemed that the figurative element had to take upon itself Europe's bad conscience and from now on the human figure appears degraded, wasted, and about to disintegrate as in Francis Bacon — a crumbling which was to extend to painting and sculpture at the end of the

1950s in Fontana, Tàpies and Burri, and to art in general in the course of the following decade.

Henri Laurens' *Autumn* represents the end result of his research into the power of expression of full forms. Basing himself on Cubist discoveries, he tried to escape from the anatomical limits of the organism without breaking its natural cohesion. Giacometti said of Laurens' style of sculpture that 'It is one of the few that reproduces what I feel when confronted with the living reality and in that way I feel it is a good likeness'.

Roger Bissière completely rethought his conception of painting. In art he sought the freshness of approximation and in order to achieve that effect he imitated children's drawings. Etienne-Martin embarked on a conscious reconstruction of the house where he spent his childhood on the basis of his impressions and emotions. This childhood memory asserted itself as an imperative as his works proceeded. At a certain point *The Overcoat* was to become the synthesis of his research, since it was a reconstruction which could be worn like a garment. With a more spontaneous primitivism the Cobra group founded by Asger Jorn sought a creativity which was deliberately undisciplined. This conception was to apply to Zoltan Kemeny and especially to Jean Dubuffet who was the author of statements which expressed his contempt for art and culture. He adopted a childlike simplicity, naive and cruel. He was immensely interested in anything that was considered stupid and dirty or mere tricks or craft. The portrait of his writer friend André

Maria-Elena
Vieira da Silva
Lisbon, 1908
Game of Chess, 1943
Oil on canvas
81 x 100
Purchased by
the State, 1947
AM 4014 P.

Dhôtel Nuancé d'Abricot has the incongruous appearance of a design made with a fork in a plate of puree. The result does not lend itself to art criticism and violates the canons of ideal beauty which were gradually being rebuilt. He created his own universe, invented characters and landscapes peopled with animals which crowded out of his imagination. At the end of the 1950s he discovered that matter in the raw, earth made up of thousands of decomposing elements, also has life. It may not be its own life but that of the wind, plants and the things that have passed over it — a rich life and at least as exciting as that of the faces of his fellow men. Later he noted that from this shapelessness could be extracted figures which are strung together endlessly, which interlock and express everything. He gives a name to this providential language: *L'Hourloupe*. Sculptures, pictures and environments follow on one after the other. His *Winter Garden* now housed in the Museum has all the attraction of a softly luminous shell, full and serene, in which the notions of top and bottom have become blurred.

At the end of the 1950s geometric art experienced a new blossoming to produce Optical Art. Victor Vasarely and François Morellet moved on from a geometric style of painting which had become respected and was part of the continuing Bauhaus tradition, to works in which the use of optical effects produced the illusion of movement. Contemporary acclaim, however, was directed primarily to Action Painting and Abstract Expressionism. This was in response to a need for commitment by gestures and action rather than by thought because action was directly involved in the production of the work. This abstraction very soon spread over Europe and America, although its best productions seemed to be localized in France — with Hans Hartung, even Pierre Soulages — and above all in the United States with Jackson Pollock. In Europe, however, awareness of the significance of the new situation in America was belated. Its influence was to be felt strongly from the end of the 1960s onwards.

Pollock painted on very large canvases laid on the ground by letting liquid paint drop on them, trying to cover the whole of the surface of the canvas by guiding the flow. This technique enabled him to create, in these interlacing threads of colour, a sensitive and fleeting figuration, that becomes increasingly apparent in his last paintings such as *The Deep*. Barnett Newman also used very large formats in his late works. The Museum has two examples of the first importance: *Shining forth (To George)* and *Jericho*. The format of the picture, the verticals and the colours create a tension which itself has the effect of an all-embracing, harmonious physical presence. Rothko achieves similar effects by less austere means.

It was by rejecting a kind of abstraction which had become 'international good taste' that a few young American artists produced works which came to be known as Pop Art. When it became an official art, the post-war abstraction lost a great deal of its vitality and attraction. The best works were being submerged in the flood of mediocre ones. In order to achieve greater verisimilitude, Pop Artists made use of signs and symbols. In some cases real objects were integrated and stuck on in a deliberately neu-

Roger Bissière
Villeréal, 1886 - Boissiérette, 1964
Black Venus, 1945
Oil on canvas with reliefs in painted stucco
100 x 80
Purchased by CNAC GP, 1983
AM 1983-463.

tral fashion. Andy Warhol was even less involved in the production of his works. Perhaps in disgust with the subjectivity of the artist, brush in hand, he took objects and pictures from newspapers and big stores, and exhibited them. He realized that current consumer goods and advertisements had a strong life because they were reproduced in their millions and on thousands of occasions. He produced works mechanically by the process of serigraphy. Already they were no longer the place where the personality of the artist was to be freely expressed — he now intervened only to select as had been the case with Marcel Duchamp. Pop Art sought to show the interest and beauty of objects in the daily environment. At first it was scorned by the critics but had its hour of glory with the award of the Venice Biennale to Robert Rauschenberg in 1964. This was the first time that the highest award in the sphere

JEAN DUBUFFET
Le Havre, 1901 - Paris, 1985
Dhôtel Nuancé d'Abricot, 1947
Oil on canvas
116 x 89
Purchased by CNAC GP with the assistance
of the Scaler Foundation, 1981
AM 1981-501.

KAREL APPEL
Amsterdam, 1921
Questioning Children, 1948
Oil-painted wooden pieces nailed to panel
85 x 56
Purchased by CNAC GP, 1985
AM 1985-128.

BRAM VAN VELDE
Zoeterwoude (Holland), 1895 - Grimaud, 1981
Composition, 1949
Oil on canvas
162.1 x 130.2
Purchased by CNAC GP, 1982
AM 1982-430.

AUGUSTE HERBIN
Quiévy, 1882 - Paris, 1960
'Vendredi' I, 1951
Oil on canvas
96 x 129
Purchased by CNAC GP, 1976
AM 1976-6.

SERGE POLIAKOFF
Moscow, 1900 - Paris, 1969
Grey and Black Composition, 1951
Oil on canvas
116 x 89
Purchased by CNAC GP, 1984
AM 1984-313.

NICOLAS DE STAËL
Saint Petersburg, 1914 - Antibes, 1955
Composition 'The Roofs', 1952
Oil on hardboard
200 x 150
Donated by the artist to the State, 1952
AM 3159 P.

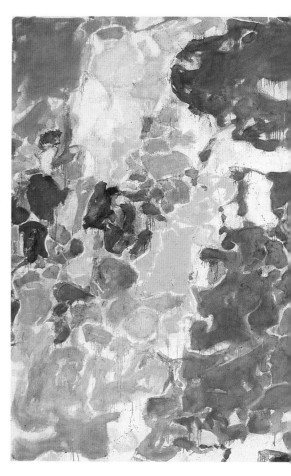

VICTOR VASARELY
Pecs (Hungary), 1908
Our IV, 1953-1964
Oil on canvas
124 x 92
Donated by the artist, 1977
AM 1977-225.

SAM FRANCIS
San Mateo (USA), 1923
In Lovely Blueness, 1955-1957
Oil on canvas
300 x 700
Donated by the Scaler Foundation, 1977
AM 1977-207.

ALBERTO MAGNELLI
Florence, 1888 - Paris, 1971
Balance, 1958
Oil on canvas
168 x 200
Purchased by the State, 1972
AM 1980-414.

FRANCIS BACON
Dublin, 1909
Van Gogh in a Landscape, 1957
Oil on canvas
153 x 120
Purchased by CNAC GP, 1982
AM 1982-2.

JACKSON POLLOCK
Cody (USA), 1912 - Southampton, 1956
The Deep, 1953
Oil on canvas
220.4 x 150.2
Donated by the Menil Foundation, 1975
AM 1976-1230.

HANS HARTUNG
Leipzig, 1904
T 1956-14, 1956
Oil on canvas
180 x 136
Donated by the Galerie de France, 1976
AM 1977-550.

ASGER JORN
Vejrun (Denmark), 1914 - Aarhus, 1973
Dovre Gubben (Poor Gubben), 1959
Oil on canvas
129 x 80
Purchased by CNAC GP, 1981
AM 1981-19.

PIERRE ALECHINSKY
Brussels, 1927
In the Land of Ink, 1959
Indian ink and distemper on paper
glued to canvas
152 x 240
Purchased by the State, 1960
AM 3989 P.

DADO
Cetinjie (Yugoslavia), 1933
The Massacre of the Innocents, 1958/59
Oil on canvas
194 x 259.5
Donated by the Scaler Foundation, 1978
AM 1978-744.

JEAN DUBUFFET
Le Havre, 1901 - Paris, 1985
Messe de Terre, 1959/60
Papier mâché glued to wood
150 x 195
Donated by Fonds DBC, 1977
AM 1977-209.

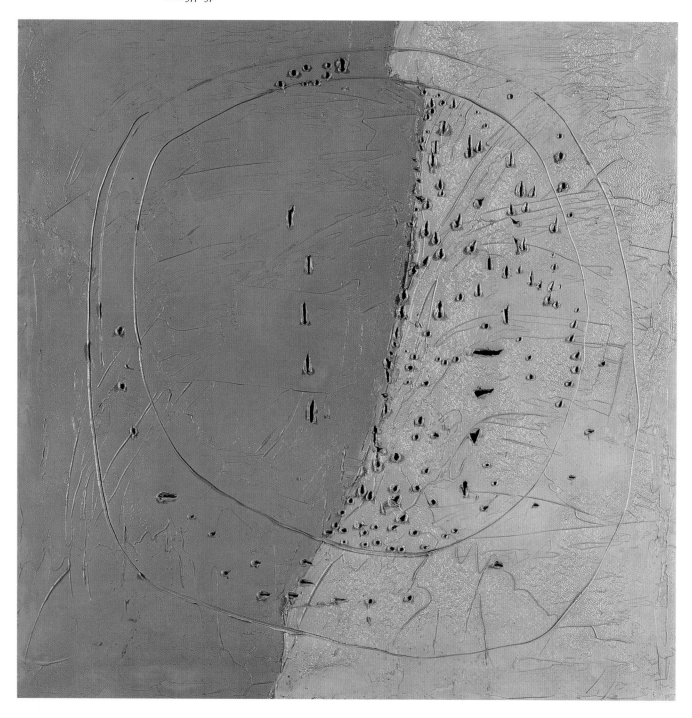

RAYMOND HAINS
Saint-Brieux, 1926
Hoarding, 1960
Collage, slashed posters on zinc
200 x 150
Trust by FNAC, 1976
AM 1976-DEP. 19.

BERNARD RÉQUICHOT
Asnières-sur-Vegre, 1929 - Paris, 1961
Portrait, 1961
Oil on canvas glued to paper and shaped
84 x 32 x 21
Donated by the Fonds DBC to the State, 1976
AM 1976-536.

ARMAND-PIERRE ARMAN
Nice, 1928
Home, Sweet Home, 1960
Assemblage of gas masks
160 x 140.5 x 20.3
Purchased by CNAC GP with the assistance of the Scaler
Foundation, 1986
AM 1986-52.

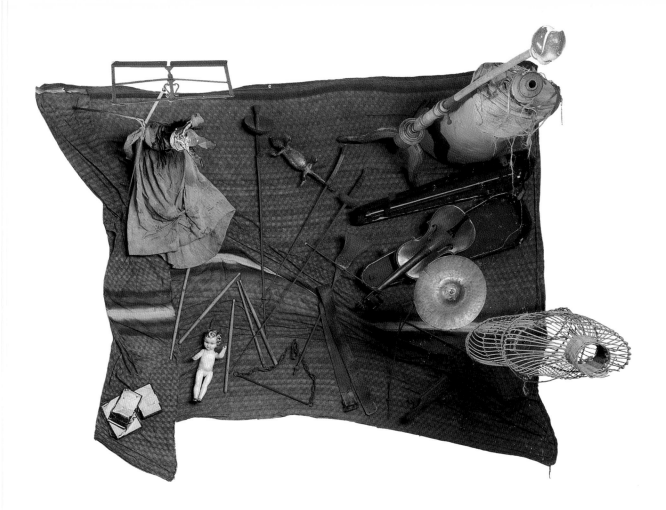

DANIEL SPOERRI
Galati (Rumania), 1930
Flea Market, 1961
Assemblage of various objects
172 x 222 x 130
Purchased by CNAC GP, 1976
AM 1976-261.

NIKI DE SAINT-PHALLE
Neuilly-sur-Seine, 1930
Crucifixion, 1963
Assemblage of various objects on painted polyester
236 x 147 x 61.5
Purchased by the Musées Nationaux, 1975
AM 1975-86.

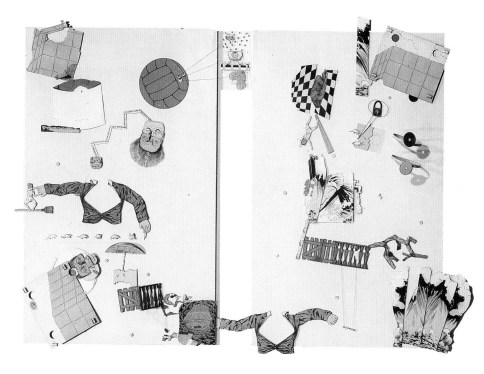

OYVIND FAHLSTRÖM
São Paulo, 1928 - Stockholm, 1976
The Cold War, 1963-1965
Variable diptych: tempera on steel and
plastic material
245 x 154
Purchased by CNAC GP, 1980
AM 1980-524.

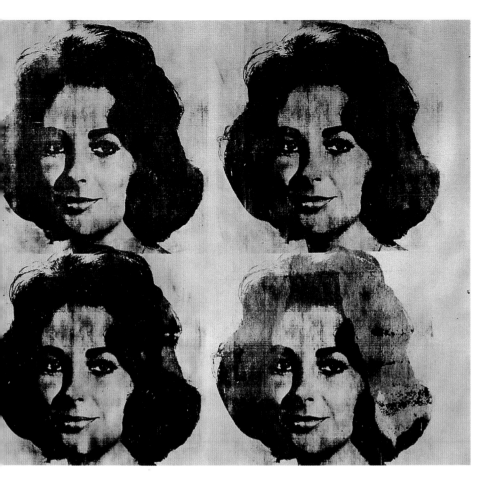

ANDY WARHOL
Pittsburgh, 1928 - New York, 1987
Ten Lizes, 1963
Oil and lacquer on canvas (serigraphic process)
201 x 564.5
Purchased by CNAC GP, 1986
AM 1986-82.

ROBERT RAUSCHENBERG
Port Arthur (USA), 1925
Oracle, 1962-1965
Installation: bath-tub, staircase, upright of window,
car door
236 x 450 x 400
Donated by M. and Mme Pierre Schlumberger, 1976
AM 1976-591.

JEAN DUBUFFET
Le Havre, 1901 - Paris, 1985
Winter Garden, 1968-1970
Environment: polyurethane on epoxy resin
480 x 960 x 550
Purchased by the State, 1973
AM 1977-251.

CLAES OLDENBURG   ▷
Stockholm, 1929
Ghost Drum Set, 1972
Installation: 10 elements in stitched and painted canvas,
polystyrene granules
80 x 183 x 183
Donated by the Menil Foundation in memory of Jean de
Menil, 1975
AM 1975-64.

TAKIS
Athens, 1925
Magnetic Wall 9 (red), 1961-1972
Acrylic on canvas, incorporating
three magnets, four cones and kite
180 x 220 x 10
Donated by the artist and the Friends
of CNAC GP, 1976
AM 1976-1237.

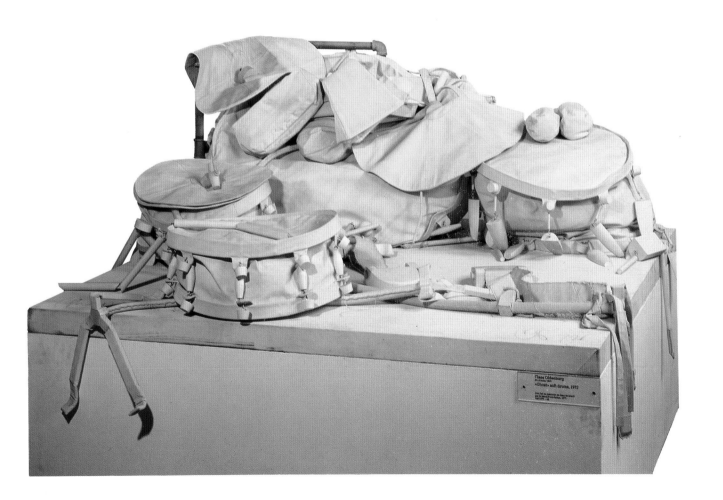

BARNETT NEWMAN
New York, 1905 - New York, 1970
Jericho, 1968/69
Acrylic on canvas
268.5 x 286
Purchased by CNAC GP with the assistance
of B. & E. Goulandris, 1986
AM 1986-272.

Contemporary Art

Around 1960 contemporary abstract art and Action Painting no longer frightened the museums. It had become a refined object of delight. But the pleasure it gave seemed suspect to many young artists. Their doubts led them to deride it and they began to question the facile notion of art for art's sake. The questions and doubts were numerous and insistent and grew in number all through this period which lasted more than ten years. They led to fundamental research on the function of art and the artist. To the traditional means of painting and sculpture were added other forms already envisaged by the avant-garde of the beginning of the century, forms already established by Cubist collage and Dada. Their revived use allowed aggressive criticism of the traditional conception of art. An explosion of categories was being witnessed whose effects are still very noticeable today.

Artists from different countries, who did not want to be tied down and reduced by a label, formed the group *Fluxus* in Germany. They chose to maintain an unstable relationship with reality. That is why their works are so diverse and totally uncaring about lasting fame. They are concerned only with the present. The future is not worth mentioning. As the word *Fluxus* indicates, these artists were seeking to bring out every facet of movement by rejecting everything that was ossified and which they associated with death. They wanted an interpenetration of art and life, of fantasy and seriousness, of comic and tragic.

Midway between object and animal, the piano in *Infiltration homogen für Konzertflügel* has a red cross sewn on the flank. In his installations and his performances Beuys often expressed a situation of anguish, a kind of inward violence capable of modi-

JOSEPH BEUYS
Kleve (West-Germany), 1921 - Düsseldorf, 1986
Infiltration homogen für Konzertflügel, 1966
Piano covered in felt and fabric
100 x 152 x 240
Purchased by CNAC GP, 1975
AM 1976-7.

Background VII/2, 1967-1984
Installation: eight piles, layers of felt,
plaques, rods, copper ribbons
196 x 455 x 643
Purchased by CNAC GP, 1985
AM 1985-139.

Häutung, 1984
Felt and fabric cross
100 x 152 x 240
Purchased by CNAC GP, 1985
AM 1985-23.

fying the perception of things in a distressed universe. This object which can be seen successively as an allegory of stifled beauty (and art) or an expression of the tragic destiny of Germany (the only subject that could until recently be tolerated with a German artist), probably has a more universal scope. Beuys' political commitment forbids us to think that this is merely a strange and beautiful object, heavily symbolic, but without any bearing on the outside world. In 1966 this piece was produced for a performance of the same name entitled 'Homogeneous infiltration for Concert Grand, the greatest contemporary composer is the thalidomide child'. The target of his derision was the cruelty of a collective poisoning which filled the news headlines. Beuys' works were conceived as the tools of political struggle extended to man's relationship with his social, historical, ecological, and human environment. They do not for this reason lose any of their plastic quality; the one is inseparable from the other. Next to it is the former worn 'skin' of the instrument hung at the artist's request.

BEN
Naples, 1935
Ben's Shop, 1958-1973
Assemblage: reconstruction of Ben's shop in Nice; various elements
350 x 500 x 350
Purchased by CNAC GP, 1975
AM 1975-185.

Seven Child-like Uses of War Material by Robert Filliou modifies the function of objects following the example of children. He renames and changes, without transforming them, a chair or a picture frame into arms of war — at the same time giving the picture of the future devastation.

Ben, who also belonged to *Fluxus*, sold records, books and other things in a tiny shop covered inside and out with strips bearing pieces of advice and short aphorisms. The result is an infinite source of entertainment, at once comic and serious. One's gaze moves over his rounded handwriting, from a pressing invitation to touch and to act to acid remarks on art and art lovers, and antipathetic to the latter's habits and weaknesses.

Some artists express in their work a scathing sharpness similar to that of Dada, which had been to some extent forgotten about since Surrealism. This tendency to irony and scepticism, encouraged by *Fluxus* had a varying but seemingly inexhaustible success and one which, to judge by the paintings of Erró, the pictures of Sigmar Polke or the *charge-objets* and paintings of Jean-Michel Sanejouand shows no signs of declining.

From another point of view, the Minimalist American artists produced 'works in which the concept is the machine which dominates everything'. Their rudimentary forms sprang from geometric models, from Russian Constructivism, and from Brancusi. The plinth is no longer necessary since the work of art is no longer a sculpture in the classical sense nor an object. Don Judd speaks of 'specific objects' which, while losing none of their quality, are no doubt connected with sculpture, the nature of which is constantly developing.

The painter Robert Ryman painted pictures of square format with white paint. Thus he refrained from tackling problems usually associated with composition, and explores the plastic variations which are possible with a few simple technical elements such as the support, the shape of the picture and its method of attachment to the wall. The resulting variations are indeed infinite. His austere-looking paintings take on a richness as soon as the gaze rests on them. These pictures starting from almost nothing make possible a reduction in formal vocabulary. The traces of the brushstrokes, their direction and the velvetiness of the material are from then on enough in the way of plastic qualities.

For Richard Serra the question of balance is the basis of sculpture. He introduces a relationship of tension and unease between the plastic object and the spectator, who is filled with an ambiguous feeling of menace and precarious balance.

A parallel development was taking place in Italy, later to be named Arte Povera. With crude and raw materials which until then had been incompatible with the refinements of artistic expression, a number of artists were grouped round a similar conception of art, inspired by the approach of Lucio Fontana. They were seeking to render visible the invisible energy running through matter. The *Giap Igloo* by Mario Merz is a cupola made of a metallic grill, to which are fixed little bags of clay. On top, neon letters write in Italian following a spiral: SE IL NEMICO SI CONCENTRA PERDE TERRENO SE SI

DISPERDE PERDE FORZA. GIAP (If the enemy scatters, he loses his strength, if he gathers his forces, he loses ground). This maxim originally used in a military context, can be applied to the work on which it is inscribed and extended to art and everyday life. The enemy becomes the metaphor of all that is external, everything that concentrates and disperses, in other words everything that is perceptible, The igloo is one of the simplest forms of dwelling. This poetic evocation of materials is used and developed by two other artists of the same movement, Jannis Kounellis and Gilberto Zorio.

'Support-Surface' was the title of an exhibition that took place in the Musée d'Art Moderne de la Ville de Paris in 1970. It brought together works by Claude Viallat, Bernard Pagès, Louis Cane, Bernard Bioules, etc. These artists did not paint but impregnated canvases which were unprepared and not stretched on a frame. They quoted Matisse as their authority in using colour freely (divorced from any reference to the model) and also American painters such as Pollock, Rothko and Newman, whose research they wished to continue. This ephemeral group was the initiator in France of many debates on art, and its influence can still be felt in the atmosphere following May 1968.

For more than twenty years Daniel Buren had been producing paintings made of vertical bands of identical width and at identical intervals painted on different supports. On the basis of an immutable principle, he created not so much images as a motif, abstract and irreducible, which could be adapted to the most varied situations. He placed them on different supports: noticeboards, flags, carried by sandwich-men or museum caretakers and even on the back of certain works of art as in the case of *Les Formes* in 1977 which had been produced for the National Museum of Modern Art. On the backs of some selected works he hung a cloth painted in accordance with his vision and cut to the appropriate format, so that it could not be seen. A second label noted and described the work of Buren. Subsequently the artist found other applications, creating structures in three dimensions or in two, in which the inside is open to the outside and vice versa. The most important and most famous of these structures, the *Double Plateau* is in the courtyard of the Palais-Royal.

JEAN TINGUELY
Fribourg, 1925
Baluba, 1961/62
Assemblage: metal, string, plastic objects, feather, duster, Shell motor
187 x 56.5 x 45
Purchased by CNAC GP, 1982
AM 1981-851.

The 'Date paintings' of the conceptual artist On Kawara show the date of the day of their creation in the language of the place where the painting was executed. In the box containing the painting is placed a copy of that day's newspaper. On that date an inconceivable number of events took place in the life of the artist and of the world. These boxes appear to contain them and call them all up from far and near.

Christian Boltanski draws the material of his works from the real or imaginary world of the individual. He repeats gestures and retraces events as scrupulously as an archaeologist who has been at pains to exaggerate his discoveries to give verisimilitude to the reality he claims to find. This small degree of deception gives the feeling of an uncertain fiction which often draws support or anchors itself in the waters of childhood so universally experienced. Who is Christian Boltanski, who is this person whose inventory of personal objects he has drawn up? His objects and photographs could belong to any of us.

From the beginning Gerhard Richter set himself against the spontaneous subversivity of *Fluxus*. The extreme coldness of his paintings allows him to remain in the background. There are one thousand and twenty-four colours, a sampling of industrial dyes which follows no rule of distribution. It could follow millions of combinations, the visual impression would be different each time. His more recent *Abstract Pictures* link a chance composition to the colours, which although it parodies lyric abstraction, allows itself no emotion. A deliberate coldness emerges from it which is belied by the bright colours and the baroque forms of these paintings. The paintings of his compatriot Penck capture the attention in a different way. In the black and white picture in the Museum, figures occupy the total surface of the canvas creating a sort of figurative web. The lines and the differences in scale between the characters, the faces, the objects, and the signs cause the space of the picture to curve inwards, making it soft and elusive.

The beginning of the 1980s saw a new interest in traditional techniques which had often been brushed aside. After laying down their brushes the better to reflect on the nature of art, there were some who decided to take them up again to pursue this reflection. This was the case with François Rouan who today integrates human figures with 'tressages' which were at once the background and foreground of his former pictures.

Brice Marden uses the plastic language of the Minimalist artist he once was. He links material and colour to find the pleasure of a scholarly and harmonious composition painted with wax. *Thira* — the door in ancient Greek — makes explicit reference to ancient architecture and religion, in which everything is linked to the omnipresent world of the gods, a door always being a place of transition.

Malcolm Morley belongs to those who have never ceased to paint and develops towards a form of painting in which the clash of beings and objects normally separated becomes more and more violent.

Today the forms of expression in art seem to be infinite. In the contemporary rooms of the Museum, objects, installations, paintings and sculptures stand side by side with a naturalness that people no longer find surprising.

JEAN-MICHEL SANEJOUAND
Lyons, 1934
Charge-objet, 1965
Rubber and wooden box covered with stapled orange fabric
75.5 x 64.3 x 34.5
Purchased by CNAC GP from the artist, 1988
AM 1988-581.

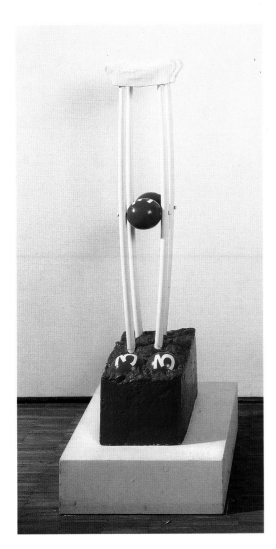

NIELE TORONI
Muralto, 1937
Brush Prints No. 50 Repeated at Regular Intervals of 30 cm, 1967
Acrylic on linen canvas
233 x 249
Purchased by CNAC GP, 1988
AM 1988-3.

JEAN-PIERRE RAYNAUD
Courbevoie, 1939
Crutches. Psycho-object, 1965
Painted plastic, wood and moleskin
105.5 x 33.5 x 23.5
Donated by Mme Jean-Claude Binoche, 1978
AM 1977-580.

On Kawara
Kariya (Aichi), 1932
Today Series (Thursday August 14, Friday August 15 and Saturday August 16 1975), 1966-1975
Liquitex on canvas and wooden box with cuttings from the *New York Times*
25.8 x 33.3 x 4.3
Purchased by CNAC GP, 1977
AM 1977-545, AM 1977-546, AM 1977-547.

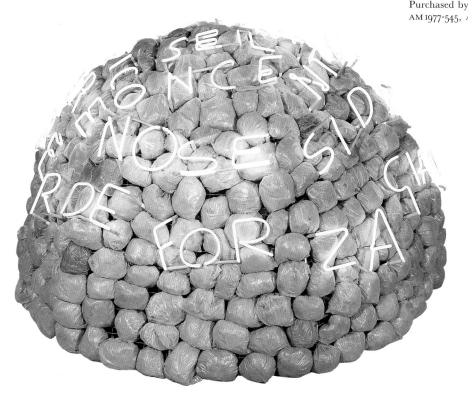

Mario Merz
Milan, 1925
Giap Igloo, 1968
Installation: iron cage, sacks of potatoes, neon, batteries, accumulators
120 x 200
Purchased by CNAC GP, 1982
AM 1982-334.

JANIS KOUNELLIS
Piraeus, 1936
Untitled, 1968
Installation: unwashed wool, string on four wooden rods
515 x 700 x 75
Purchased by CNAC GP, 1983
AM 1983-453.

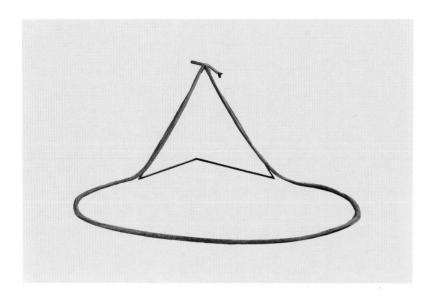

GILBERTO ZORIO
Andorno Nicca, 1944
Per Purificare le Parole, 1969
Fireman's hose, zinc nozzle, iron tubes
bent and put together
170 x 300
Purchased by CNAC GP, 1983
AM 1983-379.

BRUCE NAUMAN
Fort Wayne (USA), 1941
Dream Passage with Four Corridors, 1984
Cruciform installation
283 x 1241.5 x 1241.5
Purchased by CNAC GP, 1987
AM 1987-1136.

PANAMARENKO
Antwerp, 1940
Meganeudon I, 1971/72
Assemblage: aluminium,
balsa, Japanese silk,
epoxy. 83 x 103 x 404
Purchased by the State, 1973
AM 1980-415.

ROBERT FILLIOU
Sauve, 1926 - Les-Eyzies-de-Tayac, 1987
Seven Child-like Uses of War Material, 1970
Installation: wood, metal, glass fragments,
various objects, tools, clothing
182 x 400 x 90
Purchased by CNAC GP, 1988
AM 1988-6.

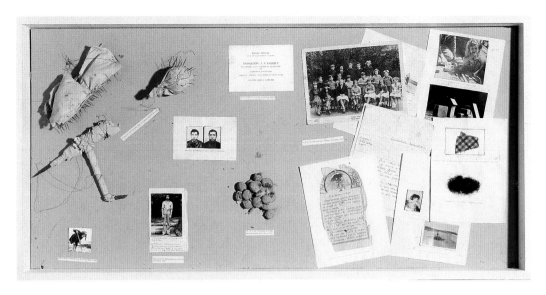

CHRISTIAN BOLTANSKI
Paris, 1944
Reference Showcase, 1971
Painted wooden box under Perspex:
photographs, hair, clothing, papers
59.6 x 120 x 12.4
Purchased by CNAC GP, 1984
AM 1984-686.

A.R. PENCK
Dresden, 1939
Untitled, 1974
Acrylic on canvas
281 x 281.8
Purchased by CNAC GP, 1982
AM 1982-333.

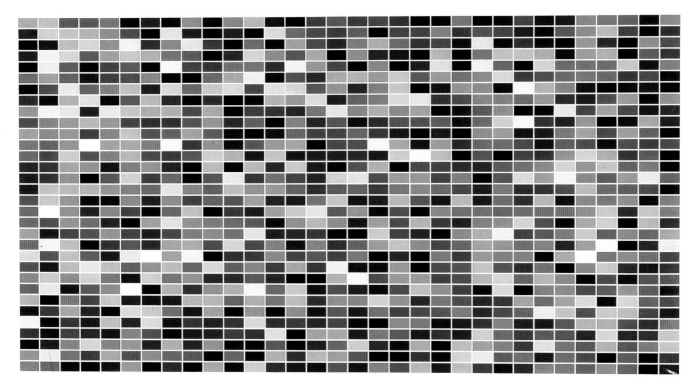

GERHARD RICHTER
Dresden, 1932
1024 Colours, No. 350/3, 1973
Lacquer on canvas
254.5 x 478
Donated by the artist, 1984
AM 1984-285.

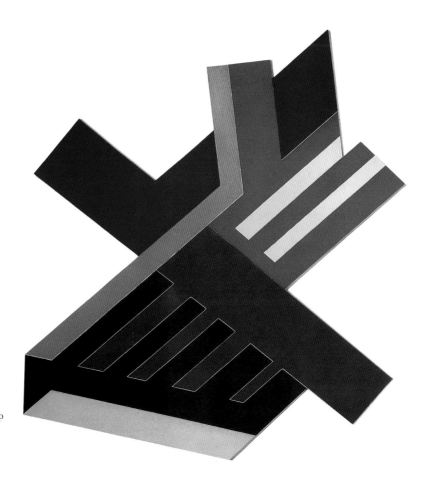

FRANK STELLA
Malden (USA), 1936
Parzeczew II, 1971
(*Polish Village Series*)
Assemblage and collage of canvas, wallpaper and cut up
felt on stretcher
285.5 x 284 x 8.2
Donated by M. and Mme Pierre Schlumberger, 1985
AM 1985-191.

JEAN LE GAC
Tamaris, 1936
Anecdotes II, a Retrospective, 1980
(series of four panels)
Colour photographs and photographs of typed texts
fixed to carbon paper
112.8 x 132.6
Purchased by CNAC GP, 1984
AM 1984-III (1-4).

CARL ANDRE
Quincy (USA), 1935
Blacks Creek, 1978
Douglas pine: five elements
122 x 183 x 30.5
Purchased by CNAC GP, 1980
AM 1980-435.

FRANÇOIS MORELLET
Cholet, 1926
Superposition and Transparency, 1980
Acrylic on two superposed canvasses
256.5 x 363
Donated by the artist, 1987
AM 1987-945.

ROBERT RYMAN
Nashville (USA), 1930
Chapter, 1981
Oil on linen canvas
223.5 x 213.5
Purchased by CNAC GP, 1982
AM 1981-850.

RICHARD SERRA
San Francisco, 1939
Corner prop No. 7 (for Nathalie), 1983
Two sheets of steel
280 x 270 x 200
Donated by the artist, 1984
AM 1984-284.

DANIEL BUREN
Boulogne-Billancourt, 1938
Eclats Peints No. 69 Vert Armor, 1985
Installation: vinyl paint on 13 elements
in window glass of various shapes
287 x 287
Purchased by CNAC GP, 1986
AM 1986-77.

BRICE MARDEN
Bronxville, 1938
Thira, 1979/80
Oil and wax on canvas (18 components)
244 x 460
Donated by the G. Pompidou Art and
Culture Foundation, 1983
AM 1983-190.

ERRÓ
Olafsvik (Iceland), 1932
Portrait of Stravinsky, 1974
(from the series *Soi sip song Bangkok*)
Oil and varnish on canvas
162.5 x 131
Purchased from the artist, 1987
AM 1987-478.

MALCOLM MORLEY
London, 1931
Cradle of Civilization with American Woman, 1982
Oil on canvas
203 x 238.5
Purchased by CNAC GP, 1987
AM 1987-558.

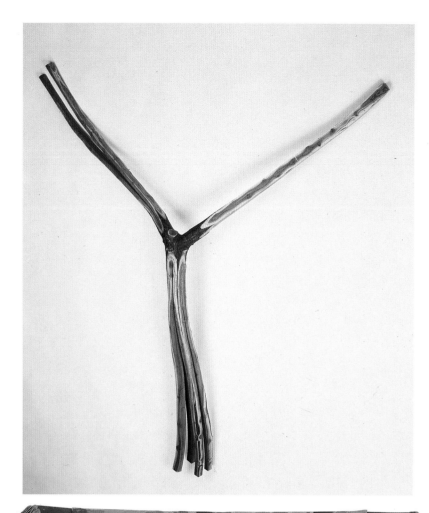

TONI GRAND
Gallarguès, 1935
Vert, Equarri, Equarri Plus une Refente Partielle,
Equarri Plus Deux Refentes Partielles, 1973
Forked branch, hewn
160 x 180
Purchased by CNAC GP, 1983
AM 1983-368.

CLAUDE VIALLAT
Nîmes, 1936
Window in Tahiti, 1976
Fabric dyes and acrylic on fringed blind
207 x 170
Purchased by CNAC GP, 1983
AM 1983-470.

FRANÇOIS ROUAN
Montpellier, 1943
Cassone VII, 1982/83
Oil on canvas
220 x 350
Purchased by CNAC GP (F. Warner gift), 1985
AM 1985-40.

Index of Artists

Page numbers in italics refer to the illustrations